GOD, GIRLS, AND GUYS

ROBIN MARSH
LAUREN NELSON

HARVEST HOUSE PUBLISHERS
EUGENE, OREGON

Robin Marsh and Lauren Nelson are represented by Working Title Agency, LLC, Spring Hill, TN.

Backcover author photo by gfellerstudio.com

Cover by Dugan Design Group, Bloomington, Minnesota

Some names and minor details have been changed in the real-life stories shared in this book to protect the privacy of the individuals mentioned.

GOD, GIRLS, AND GUYS
Copyright © 2012 by Robin Marsh and Lauren Nelson
Published by Harvest House Publishers
Eugene, Oregon 97402
www.harvesthousepublishers.com

Library of Congress Cataloging-in-Publication Data

Marsh, Robin, 1964-
   God, girls, and guys / Robin Marsh and Lauren Nelson with Kelly King.
      p. cm.
   ISBN 978-0-7369-4523-3 (pbk.)
   ISBN 978-0-7369-4524-0 (eBook)
   1. Man–woman relationships—Religious aspects—Christianity. 2. Man–woman relationships—Biblical teaching. 3. Dating (Social customs)—Religious aspects—Christianity. 4. Teenage girls—Sexual behavior. 5. Teenage girls—Religious life. I. Nelson, Lauren, 1986– II. King, Kelly. III. Title.
   BT705.8.M37 2012
   241'.66408352—dc23
                                                                                    2012001365

Printed in the United States of America

12 13 14 15 16 17 18 19 20 / VP-KBD / 10 9 8 7 6 5 4 3 2 1

Contributing Writer

Kelly King's special touch as a contributing writer helped make *God, Girls, and Guys* a great resource to help teens navigate the often tumultuous world of dating and relationships. She's also reached out to teens for more than 25 years by teaming up with her husband, Vic, to work with the youth in their local church. Kelly has published numerous articles, discipleship materials, and student ministry curricula. She currently serves as women's specialist for the Baptist General Convention in Oklahoma, where she encourages women to embrace and echo God's heart. Kelly, Vic, and their college-aged children enjoy hiking and fishing.

Acknowledgments

Kelly, thank you for your hard work, wisdom, and willing heart to see lives changed. We love you and are so grateful for your help in making this book happen.

Thank you, *Bill Reeves,* for your insights and ability to answer all our questions. We appreciate having you for a literary agent.

The Harvest House team—especially Bob Hawkins, LaRae Weikert, Hope Lyda, and Barb Gordon—we thank you for your support in our vision to see lives changed by helping people know the Lord.

Dr. Alan Day, Dr. Michael Catt, Dr. Anthony Jordan, and *Dr. Ted Kersh*— we appreciate your lifework as pastors to help us and so many others come to know the life-changing power found in the Word of God. Thank you for your support and encouragement in our ministry to share God's Good News with teens.

And, most important, to our Lord and Savior, *Jesus Christ.* You are our everything. We pray this book brings glory and honor to You.

CONTENTS

AH, LOVE....

It's not an accident this book has landed in your hands. God has you reading this for a reason. Maybe you picked it up because you're curious about guys and what makes them tick. Perhaps you've been praying about how to have a godly relationship. Maybe your mom or grandmother gave you this book because they would love to pour wise advice about guys into your head. In their quest to impart wisdom, they may figure if you don't listen to them, you might read this. Plus it might avoid those awkward mother–daughter dating talks.

Whatever the reason or however you got the book, God's Word has a lot to say about relationships. Our hope is that through reading this book and examining God's Word, you will fall in love with the Lord Jesus. We pray that you will come to know the Savior in a deeper, more intimate way. Through a closer relationship with the heavenly Father, we believe your earthly relationships will be healthier and stronger.

So let's get started by introducing ourselves.

Robin Marsh: I'm the mom of a young man named Cade, and my husband, Keith, is the love of my life. I've gone through the joys of relationships, and before I met Keith, I experienced some pretty dark hours as a serious relationship broke up. In the midst of good and bad, God has been incredibly faithful to me. He's given me a passion to share my story, along with the truths I've learned, and, more importantly, I get to share His story with you.

I've been in the television news broadcasting business for almost 30 years. My alarm clock goes off each weekday morning at 3:00 (yes, a.m.!), and I make my way to work at the CBS affiliate KWTV-News 9 in Oklahoma City to anchor the morning news. It's an exciting career because every day is different.

I never dreamed how my life would change after I was assigned to interview Miss America in 2007. Her name is Lauren Nelson.

Lauren Nelson: Most people know me because I was privileged to wear the Miss America crown in 2007. I met Robin when she interviewed me, and since then our friendship has blossomed. She's mentored me professionally and spiritually. She even introduced me to my husband!

Randy and I have been married for several years. We don't have any children yet, but we plan to. We live in Oklahoma City.

I am also in the television news business, and I currently anchor the afternoon newscast on KWTV-News 9.

God has given me a love for helping girls understand their true identity in Christ. As this passion has increased, so have opportunities to serve. In the past year I've confirmed what God was doing in my heart by totally giving my life to Him. Through this commitment, God has opened doors for me to share His love and life-changing message with you and other girls.

Our friendship and ministry: We are great friends who share an enthusiasm to minister to teen girls. We enjoyed writing our first book for teens, *God, Girls, and Getting Connected,* and it's helping a lot of girls find answers to questions about life, faith, and relationships. In *God, Girls, and Guys* we answer questions you have about dating and cover a lot of issues surrounding dating relationships, including how it is a reflection of your relationship with Christ.

We examine a lot of truths without throwing a lot of do's and don'ts at you. We've also included some of our personal stories to give you a glimpse of who we are. We share the good choices we've made as well as some of the ones we wish we could take back.

Our desire is to encourage you. Our prayer is that you will begin to rely more and more on God to guide your relationships. We know that without a relationship with Him and His guidance, no guy/girl relationship can be solid.

We want you to know that we're far from perfect. We've had our share of guy disasters, but we survived them. And, thankfully, we're both married to really terrific, godly husbands.

One more thing: We're not psychologists who have guys totally figured out. (Is there anyone who has?) The topic of guys triggers a lot of questions for girls and women because, just like us, no two guys are alike. However, what we've found is that there is a great resource for ultimate wisdom and truth—God's Word. We love God's stories about relationships and what we can learn from them. While dating isn't a concept we find in the Old Testament, we do find great examples of relationships throughout the entire Bible that we can look to for guidance. Some of the stories are beautiful love stories. Some of them contain abuse and heartache. Fortunately, we can learn from both.

Our Journey with You

We've found in looking at other books that while some Christians offer great advice, there's no better way to find wisdom than digging into God's Word.

At the end of each chapter you'll find some personal reflection questions to help you take the step from reading the words on the page to applying them to your life. The questions aren't tests to see whether you've read the chapter. They are ways for you to think about the information on a deeper and more personal level.

We've included a "Small Group Leader's Guide" at the end of the book that you'll find helpful if you study this book with other girls and a leader. We encourage you to find a female youth leader or mentor who will be your on-site relationship mentor. Even though we look at this book as our journey with you, there's great value in having a woman you can call or text when you need to talk or get specific guy guidance.

As an additional resource, we encourage you to check out our Website: www.withunveiledfaces.com. This way we can interact with you—even when you're finished reading this book.

My friend, we are praying for you as we begin this journey. We're excited about discovering what God wants to reveal about Himself and guys!

THE "L" WORD
WHAT IS LOVE?

Love: *A profoundly tender, passionate affection for another person; a feeling of warm personal attachment or deep affection, as for a parent, child, or friend; sexual passion or desire; a person toward whom love is felt; beloved person; sweetheart.*

Have you ever said "I love that movie" and "I love my necklace" in the same day? We use the word "love" in some of the silliest ways. But "love" is actually a pretty serious word. It's so serious that God uses it to describe Himself. First John 4:16 says, "We know and rely on the love God has for us. God is love. Whoever lives in love lives in God, and God in them."

Did you catch what that verse just said? Not only does love *come* from God, God *is* love. Think about that for a second. The Creator of the universe, the One who hung the stars, calls Himself love. The same word God uses to describe Himself, we use to describe our affection for fast food, shoes, our favorite sweatshirt, and the latest flick.

What's your favorite love story? Most good love stories end with the guy going to great lengths to prove his love for his girl. The leading man pursues his leading lady until she believes, beyond a doubt, that his love is real and everlasting. Do you know that you are a leading lady? God, the ultimate and only true leading man, is pursuing your heart this very minute. To show His longing to have a relationship with you, He sent His Son from heaven to live, to die, and to be resurrected on earth so you wouldn't need to ever question His lasting love and commitment. We pray that you'll discover the true meaning of love as you celebrate your role as God's leading lady—a young woman worth knowing, pursuing, and embracing.

Maybe you've had feelings for a guy or you've wished a particular guy loved you. That's one kind of love, but we want you to discover how love is even more significant and life-changing than a feeling that goes up and down. Love is the motivation for how you treat everyone in your world. With God at the center of all your relationships, including the ones between you and guys, you and your parents, you and your friends, and even you and people you don't know, your life will be more fulfilling and significant.

Do you know that many of the stories in the Bible are love stories? That's why we are going to highlight a few of them throughout this book. They reveal how to love...and sometimes how *not* to love. They also let us in on a very great secret: When we place God in the center of our universe, we'll be inspired and guided to strengthen all the connections we have. You see—God's love is life-changing and forever!

But let's start at the beginning. Immerse yourself in God's great love for you. Then you'll know and experience what love really is, and you'll know what kind of love you want in a relationship with a guy.

The First Love Story

To look at the beginning of love, let's visit Adam and Eve in the Garden of Eden. By exploring the creation story found in Genesis 1 and 2, you can see how God created man and woman and desired for them to have a relationship with each other—for friendship, affection, and, yes, making babies. God created the heavens, the earth, the animals, day and night, and then Adam. Adam was unlike any other creature because God said, "Let us make mankind in our image, in our likeness" (Genesis 1:26). So Adam was special, lived in a perfect garden, was top dog of creation. He owned everything and even had a perfect relationship with God. Nevertheless, God saw that Adam was incomplete.

"The LORD God said, 'It is not good for the man to be alone. I will make a helper suitable for him'" (Genesis 2:18). This was the first time God said something wasn't good! God gave Adam a desire for relationship beyond the relationship they had together. So God created woman. Actually, the literal translation states that God *fashioned* woman from man. And we all enjoy a good fashion story, don't we?

Eve may have entered the garden scene after Adam, but let's get something straight. Woman was not an afterthought. We were part of

God's plan from the very beginning. He just wanted Adam to experience the need and desire for relationships with Him and with others first. The same is true for us. Down deep inside of us, God created in us the desire for relationships.

Can you remember how old you were when you first dressed up and pretended you were getting married? And how often do your conversations with friends center on guys these days? How many times have those conversations included your dreams for marriage and family? It's no coincidence that many girls share these thoughts. These are not bad things. God is the one who put those desires within you.

It's been said that God's greatest medium is His people. He uses the people He puts in our lives to help reveal His plan for us. He gave Adam the desire for relationship with another living being in the form of a woman—a person who would be his life partner on earth. Genesis 2:23-24 says, "'This is now bone of my bones and flesh of my flesh; she shall be called "woman," for she was taken out of man.' That is why a man leaves his father and mother and is united to his wife, and they become one flesh." In some Bible translations, you'll find the word "bond" used instead of "united," which implies sticking like superglue! God meant for love between man and woman to be a relationship that is closer than close. Two lives joined together. God not only showed His love for us by sending His Son to restore our relationship with Him, but He also gives us the opportunity to experience love from others on this earth. Love is a true gift from our heavenly Father.

from Robin...
Daddy's Girl

Speaking of fathers… My sister and I would both tell you we are "daddy's girls." Part of being a daddy's girl means I trust my father completely, and I am secure in his love. The security I find in the love of my dad continues today. He's demonstrated his love many times, especially during my teen years—a time when girls form some of their most important thoughts about relationships with guys.

One of my favorite dad moments happened one cold, snowy night in southwestern Oklahoma, where I grew up. I was stressed about a test the next day. My life was busy with cheerleading, barrel racing with my horse, and staying on top of all the demands of high school. My dad sensed my stress that winter night. He knew just what I needed. He threw open the door to my bedroom, hurled a snowball at me, and said, "Hey, Robi Jo, it's time for a snowball fight!" Instead of adding to the pressure I was feeling, he lightened my load as we went outside and played in the snow in the middle of the night. That memory still makes me smile!

Being a daddy's girl also means I knew I could count on him when I needed a safe place. Our household policy was always "Call anytime, no questions asked." That policy came in handy one Saturday night when I was hanging out with some friends who decided to stop at a party. As I stepped inside the house, I was immediately uncomfortable. I knew I wasn't where I was supposed to be. I didn't have my own car, so I felt trapped. Thankfully, I thought about our house policy. So I called my dad. And he came to my rescue—no questions asked, just like my parents had promised. I was relieved I had a father who was willing to support me and protect me.

Trust. Protection. Security. Those are all things we want from our daddies. And believe me, I realize not all girls have this kind of earthly father. You might have read that last paragraph and said, "I don't even have a dad at home. I have no idea what she's talking about." You might also be wondering what this story has to do with boys and relationships. It has everything to do with relationships and how you view guys in general. Why? Because no matter what your relationship is like with your earthly father, there is a heavenly Father who loves you even more! The first time I heard those words, I was blown away. I began to see how much God loved me, and I started to understand the true concept of the "L" word. I embraced what absolute trust and protection meant—that Jesus would *never* leave me. And I felt the ultimate security by realizing that God promised abundant life in this life *and* for eternity. I knew I was forever my heavenly Daddy's girl.

How about you? Are you a Daddy's girl? *Mae?*

What Is "True" Love?

Most girls we know love Disney movies. Maybe you've watched a few—especially the princess stories of young fair maidens waiting for their one true love. One of our favorites is *Enchanted*, a movie that parodies many classic princess stories. The young, animated Giselle is waiting on her one true love when she's cast into the reality of modern-day New York City. Her perfect environment of singing animals and awaiting true love's kiss is instantly dashed when she finds herself stranded in a rainstorm on the sidewalk of a noisy city. Joyfully, by the end of the story, Giselle finds her true love and all ends happily ever after.

As nice as it may seem, true love is not like that. It's not singing birds and glass slippers. Love is an action, and the ultimate act of love happened more than 2,000 years ago when Jesus stood in our place and died on the cross for our sin. That's true love and devotion.

The Language of Love

"Love" is a little word with a big meaning. Most of the Old Testament was originally written in Hebrew, where "love" is used as a verb and a noun (remember grammar class?). You probably relate to the action or verb form of love most, which is derived from the Hebrew word *'ahab,* meaning a strong emotional attachment to someone, such as family or romantic relationships. It's a strong attachment someone might have toward another person.

The New Testament was written in Greek and two words used for love are *phileo* and *agape. Philio* is often described as "brotherly love." Ever wonder why Philadelphia is called the city of brotherly love? You got it! It came right out of the Greek word for love. *Phileo* love includes the love you feel for your sister, your brother, and your friends.

The Greek word most often used to describe Christian love is *agape.* Even the word *agape* is used in different ways in the New Testament. Sometimes it describes the love God has toward His Son, Jesus Christ, and to the human race. It's also used to describe the way God wants us to treat others. But perhaps the most important way it's used is to describe the nature of God. What does that mean? That love can be known *from an action,* primarily the action God chose when He gave us the gift of sending His Son, Jesus Christ, to die in our place for our sin.

What Love Is Not

What society says love is and what God says about love are worlds apart. Here are some myths we've observed in worldly views of love:

True love: One of the best descriptions of agape love is found in 1 Corinthians 13:4-8. The apostle Paul describes what true love looks like. Read the words carefully and compare how Paul describes love and what your relationships are like.

"Love is patient, love is kind. It does not envy, it does not boast, it is not proud. It does not dishonor others, it is not self-seeking, it is not easily angered, it keeps no record of wrongs. Love does not delight in evil but rejoices with the truth. It always protects, always trusts, always hopes, always perseveres. Love never fails."

Myth 1: Love isn't about what you give—it's about what you can get. Listen to people talk about relationships, and you'll hear the word "I" a lot. "*I* want to date a tall guy," "*I* am looking for someone who will be successful," and "*I* need someone who will make me happy." "I" statements are all about what the speaker wants to get or have in a relationship. True love is not about getting. *True love is about giving.* Mark 10:45 says, "The Son of Man did not come to be served, but to serve, and to give his life as a ransom for many." Love is a selfless act, not a selfish pursuit.

Myth 2: Love means it's okay to "go all the way." Watch five minutes of most shows on TV or skim through a magazine, and you'll find that the world's version of love almost always involves sex. We'll talk about this in greater detail later, but God's Word is clear that to love someone prior to marriage means keeping him and you holy and pure.

Myth 3: Love is picket fences and perfect lives. As wonderful as it may sound, this just isn't true. No one's life is perfect, and all relationships encounter conflict. Loving someone always involves compromise, sacrifice, and, many times, an attitude of forgiveness. Love is never perfect, but that doesn't mean it isn't wonderful.

The First Time Love Is Mentioned in Scripture

We've looked at the story of Adam and Eve and how God created the guy/girl relationship to be uniquely special. But does it surprise you to know that the first time the word "love" is mentioned in the Bible is several chapters later? And it's not even about a guy and girl!

Grab your Bible and take a quick look at Genesis 22:1-18. Here's a bit of background. It's been a few generations since Adam and Eve. Scripture now focuses on the life of Abram, later called Abraham. God promises Abraham that he'll be the "father of many nations." For decades, Abraham and his wife, Sarah (Sarai), wait for the fulfillment of this promise in the form of a son, but they remain childless. They even take matters into their own hands and use Hagar, Sarah's maid, to birth Abraham's child, who was named Ishmael.

Finally, at the ripe old age of 90, Sarah becomes pregnant, and God fulfills His promise. Sarah gives birth to Isaac, whose name means "laughter." Abraham and Sarah are overjoyed. The love Abraham has for Isaac is immense, and the faith Abraham has in God soars. Then the unthinkable happens.

God tells Abraham to take Isaac and kill him as a sacrifice offering (Genesis 22). Can you imagine how Abraham must have felt? Why in the world would God take away the person He had promised? How could this make any sense? And here, for the first time, we see the word "love" mentioned. Look closely at Genesis 22:2: "God said, 'Take your son, your only son, whom you love…'" The Hebrew word translated "love" is the one we mentioned earlier: 'ahab.

If God understood how much Abraham loved Isaac, why would He ask him to sacrifice his son? While there is much to understand about the background of the son taking on the sin of the family in Hebrew culture, a simple answer is that it's a matter of Abraham trusting God. Did Abraham believe God would still fulfill His promise? Did Abraham believe God could raise Isaac from the dead if Isaac was offered as a sacrifice?

Abraham took Isaac and headed for the place God had told him to go. He took the wood needed for building a fire for the "offering." God honored Abraham's faith by eventually providing a ram as a substitute for Isaac for the sin offering. But isn't it interesting that the first mention of love involves death?

God is our heavenly Father. He can be trusted. And He loves you more than you can comprehend. In fact, this mention of love demonstrated God's love because He provided a substitute. This is a foreshadowing of God's ultimate demonstration of love when Jesus came and willingly became a sacrifice for our sin in our place. Yes, God still demonstrates His love toward us today.

from Lauren...
Knowing of God and Knowing God

I grew up in a Christian home, and my family went to church almost every week. I knew the stories of the Bible, and I knew a lot about who God was. But I didn't know Him personally. It was during this uncertain time in my faith that I was chosen to be Miss America 2007. What an unforgettable year of hard work and personal growth that was. But at the same time, I realized how lonely I felt.

At the end of this experience, I found myself handing over my crown and wanting a new start on life.

With a strong desire for change, I walked off the stage and headed straight to my hairdresser and asked him to cut my hair short. I also made the big decision to break up with my long-standing boyfriend. In the midst of living out many girls' dreams, I had never been lonelier. *wow*

On my flight home to Oklahoma, Robin was on the same plane. She had done an interview with me and my mom during my year as Miss America, so we greeted each other and had a brief conversation. I had no idea then that God was prompting Robin to pray for me.

God didn't let up on asking Robin to pray for me, so she didn't give up on me. She called me, and although I didn't respond to her right away, I eventually called her back. Robin thought I was living in Tulsa, but I actually lived just miles from her home. I'd decided to use my scholarship from the pageant to attend the University of Central Oklahoma.

Robin and I kept in contact, and our friendship quickly grew. She invited me to a Bible study in her home and welcomed me to attend her church. Soon I was going to church with her family on a regular basis.

From the beginning, I saw that Robin had a living, intimate relationship with Jesus. It seemed she was able to actually talk to God... and He listened! She was relying on Him in her daily life, and I knew she sensed His presence each day. I had never experienced that type of romantic relationship with my Creator.

During this time of growth in my faith journey, I met a wonderful man in the church named Randy. He was serving as a student associate on the staff, and I knew we had a connection that would go beyond friendship. We started dating, and I was grateful to have someone in my life who loved God.

A few months after we started dating, Randy and I attended a church event together on the Fourth of July. The church had asked me to sing during the special celebration, which also featured a compelling talk by Joe White, the founder of Kanakuk Kamps. During the time of invitation to confess one's faith, Randy leaned over and said he would go forward with me if I needed to make a decision for a closer walk with Christ. He sensed that the Holy Spirit had been working in my heart.

My first reaction was "I don't need to do that." But the longer I waited, the more the Lord worked on my heart, prompting me, "Are you going to ignore Me? Are you going to let this moment pass by?" Right then I knew God was calling me to a deeper relationship with Him. So I went forward in my faith and in my belief in a love that was bigger than anything I'd ever known. That night sparked an adventure of learning more about a personal relationship with God and growing in head and heart knowledge.

God began working more strongly in my life. I turned from some sins that had been a regular part of my life and spent more time with God and in His Word. Through this time of fostering my relationship with God, I began to see I was still holding on to some shame and guilt from things I'd done in my past.

Fast-Forward to October 2011

The Sunday morning guest speaker at church gave a very powerful message about making sure we knew we were Christians. I sat there listening with my heart in my throat and conviction gripping my innermost parts. When the preacher gave the invitation to accept the gift of salvation through Jesus, I found myself unable to leave my seat. I was needed back up on stage to lead the invitation song, but God was wanting me to pay attention. I asked God, "Didn't I already do this? What will people think? I'm one of the worship leaders!" The preacher then posed this simple question: "Can you tell the person next to you that you are 100 percent sure you are saved?" I found myself unable to do so, so I went forward. I told the congregation that I needed to know without a doubt that if I died I would go to heaven to be with Jesus. That is the time I surrendered my all—*everything* within me—and humbly gave God my life.

Love became very personal and powerful as I finally fully understood that Jesus died on the cross so I could have eternal life with Him. And He did it so I could live free from all the guilt and shame I'd been carrying around. It was the greatest decision I have ever made in my life.

I find it remarkable that Independence Day was, for me, the beginning of my dependence on the Lord. It was also the beginning of learning the true meaning of the "L" word. Yes, God was working in my life before that day, but it took me a little while to forgive myself and ask God to free me from the shame and guilt of past mistakes. I finally understood that experiencing God's love through a relationship with Christ was my first step toward truly loving others.

Are You Ready to Dive In?

So, are you ready to learn about true love? Are you ready to learn how to trust God completely? How to find security in His unfailing love for you? Let's dive in together over the next several chapters. We're going to talk about how to navigate the waters of having godly relationships with guys, and we're going to help you draw closer to the God who designed guy/girl relationships. We want all of you to be a Daddy's girl—a girl whose heart belongs to her heavenly Father.

Personal Reflections

1. How do you define "love"? Is your definition closer to the world's definition or God's?

   GOD'S

2. How has this chapter challenged your thoughts about love? What have you learned? *How similar we are that without God at the forefront we are lonely.*

3. Think about how our culture views love. How does it differ from God's design? *God's design — selfless culture's — selfish*

4. How has God demonstrated His love to you? How can you demonstrate God's love to others this week?

   He has blessed me so much — esp. His son —

5. Have you personally accepted God's invitation *yes* to follow Him? Like Lauren, do you know about God but don't have a personal relationship with Him? If this describes you, who can you talk to this week about becoming a Christian?

6. If you already have a relationship with Christ, who will you share your faith with this week? Remember, you don't have to have all the answers to be a witness for Christ. You can share something that is precious and inspiring—your own story of faith.

   Hmm.

MIRROR, MIRROR OF MY HEART

HOW DOES GOD SEE ME?

Beauty: *The combination of all the qualities of a person or thing that delights the senses and pleases the mind; a very attractive and well-formed girl or woman.*

We all love looking at them...at fashion magazines, that is. It's fun to keep up with the styles and trends. But before you skim the slick pages of your favorite one, there should be an alarm sounding in your head that says, "These pages may be hazardous to your health!" The covers are usually graced with super skinny models in expensive jeans, clever headlines for stories on how celebrities are living out fantasies, and announcements of who did and didn't make the list of the most beautiful people. Without even opening such a magazine, the messages being sent are that your self-worth is based on what you do, what you have, and what you look like.

So how is this a health hazard? It only takes a few seconds of looking at many popular magazines for most girls and women to feel worse about themselves and their bodies. One study found that 70 percent of teen girls agreed that magazines strongly influenced what they thought was the ideal body type.[1] The devastation done to our hearts and mental states can be lifelong when we compare ourselves against people we've never met using scales that aren't real. Letting other people dictate our sense of self-worth leads to a lot of insecurity.

from Robin...
A Nose for News

Since I'm in the business of anchoring the TV news, people sometimes feel free to comment on my looks. When a woman is in the public eye, it's pretty easy for people to judge her by the style of her hair, the clothes she wears, and her weight and shape. And then there is the 10-second rule. Most people holding a remote in their hand will decide in just 10 seconds if they are going to stay on that channel or switch to another program. Talk about pressure! It's easy to understand why television news anchors are often evaluated by how they look rather than the details of the stories they report.

The reality of this pressure hit me right in the nose, so to speak, when I was a young broadcaster. It was devastating to hear my news director say I really had no future in television news. Why? Was it because I didn't have the right personality? Was it because I didn't have the skills to perform the job? Nope. His rationale for potential failure was right in the middle of my face—my nose! It was harsh and hurtful to hear him say, "If you want to make it in this business, you'll have to get a nose job, Robin."

The fact of the matter is that I like my nose. It's part of my Italian heritage. My facial features include big eyes, a big smile, and, you guessed it, a big nose! I never was paranoid about my nose until my boss told me I needed surgery to be successful in broadcasting. Because of his harsh comment, I became very conscious of my looks and insecure. I had trouble being myself while doing shows on the air. I drove myself crazy worrying. My nose dominated my thoughts, and I became positive that it dominated the thoughts of viewers when they watched me.

Several months later I shared my concern with a friend. I told her I might need to alter my looks to make it in the news business. Her words have always stayed with me. She said, "Every great face has a great flaw." That was when I began to understand how God had uniquely created me. I learned from His Word that true beauty comes from Christ living inside me, not from what people think about my physical appearance. Uniqueness is something to be proud of.

After almost 30 years in television broadcasting, I still have a "nose for news." Now, more than ever, I'm grateful for the nose God gave me! I've learned there's much more to beauty than the standards the world gives.

Reality Check

In 2006, Dove, the skincare products company, produced a commercial that went viral on YouTube. More than 3.5 million people watched the short, fast-paced video that portrays how beauty has been distorted in our culture. The video shows a clean-faced model who is not only transformed by makeup and hairstylists, but she is then "enhanced" by computer techniques to boost her beauty to a physically unattainable level.

Most of us would love it if everyone saw us through the lens of Photoshop possibilities. But the reality is that physical beauty is exactly as the old saying describes: "skin deep."

How many times do you look in the mirror each day? A few years ago, a survey in Liverpool revealed that the average number of times a woman stopped to look at herself in a mirror was 71 times a day. The survey also noted that women put on lipstick or touched up their makeup at least 11 times a day. Even if we stopped by a mirror 34 times, that means most of us check ourselves out every 30 minutes![2]

Another area of potential stigma for girls is their bodies. Many girls place great importance on how much they weigh or how their bodies are proportioned. The average height for most women in the United States is around 5'2", and the average body wears a size 10 or 12. The models you see in your favorite magazines? They are probably close to 6' tall and wear no larger than a size 4. Talk about unrealistic expectations.

Have you felt the pressure to have a certain body type or size? As we learn more about God's love, we pray you will also discover how to see yourself as God sees you. It is such a gift to embrace your beauty and preciousness as God intended.

The Mirror of Your Heart

Recently, the world population hit the 7 billion mark. That's a lot of people who all possess a God-given uniqueness, which includes physical appearance. Even if you're an identical twin, there are no two people who are exactly alike. It's so amazing when you consider God's creativity and purpose in the way He uniquely designed us.

A great passage in Scripture that describes God's handiwork in designing you is found in Psalm 139. David's words express God's unique knowledge of you and His special care in your creation. Read Psalm 139:13-18 and replace every personal pronoun with your name, just like we did with Lauren's name:

> [LORD,] you created *Lauren's* inmost being; you knit *Lauren* together in *Lauren's* mother's womb. *Lauren* praises you because *Lauren* is fearfully and wonderfully made; your works are wonderful. *Lauren* knows that full well. *Lauren's* frame was not hidden from you when *Lauren* was made in the secret place, when *Lauren* was woven together in the depths of the earth. Your eyes saw *Lauren's* unformed body; all the days ordained for *Lauren* were written in your book before one of them came to be. How precious to *Lauren* are your thoughts, God! How vast is the sum of them! Were *Lauren* to count them, they would outnumber the grains of sand—when *Lauren* is awake, *Lauren* is still with you.

Your turn!

> [LORD,] you created Maddy inmost being; you knit Maddy together in Maddy mother's womb. Maddy praises you because Maddy is fearfully and wonderfully made; your works are wonderful. Maddy knows that full well. Maddy frame was not hidden from you when Maddy was made in the secret place, when Maddy was woven together in the depths of the earth. Your eyes saw Maddy unformed body; all the days ordained for Maddy were written in your book before one of them came to be. How precious to Maddy are your thoughts, God! How vast is the sum of them! Were Maddy to count them, they would outnumber the grains of sand—when Maddy is awake, Maddy is still with you.

When you read the verses this way, how does it change your attitude about yourself? How does it help you better understand how God sees you? These verses confirm that God uniquely created you, He loves you, He shapes your life, and He uses you for His glory.

The way you see yourself reflects your attitude toward the way God created you. You can complain and be negative or you can be thankful. What about the way God created you are you thankful for? When you learn to look in the mirror and recognize the beauty of God's handiwork, you'll become more confident. When you're confident and secure in who God made you to be and how He made you, that is the first step in preparing your heart for relationships with guys.

Makeup and Cute Clothes Aren't Bad

We want to make something clear up front. While both of us emphasize that inner beauty is the most important thing to achieve, we're not saying you shouldn't take care of yourself. We enjoy looking our best and shopping for cute clothes too. Celebrating your inner beauty doesn't mean you should fill your body with junk food or avoid showers.

God has given you an outer body that requires attention. Sometimes the way you care for yourself on the outside is a reflection of how you take care of yourself on the inside. First Corinthians 6:19-20 says, "Do you not know that your bodies are temples of the Holy Spirit, who is in you, whom you have received from God? You are not your own; you were bought at a price. Therefore honor God with your bodies." These verses speak not only to honoring God by being sexually pure, but also by taking good care of your physical body.

God also gave you a spiritual, inner self that requires attention. Becoming beautiful on the inside doesn't happen overnight. Spiritual beauty takes discipline. How much time do you spend in God's Word compared to the time you spend putting on your makeup? Read Paul's instructions to Timothy: "Have nothing to do with godless myths and old wives' tales; rather, train yourself to be godly. For physical training is of some value, but godliness has value for all things, holding promise for both the present life and the life to come" (1 Timothy 4:7-8). The word "train" is translated from the Greek word *gumnazo*, which is also where we get our word "gymnasium." Just like you physically train yourself in a gym, spiritual training takes time and effort.

from Lauren...

Crowning Moment

I grew up watching the Miss America Pageant. All those beautiful women on stage…I was in awe of their grace and poise. In my wildest dreams, I never believed I could ever be one of those beautiful people, much less become the pinnacle—Miss America.

My pageant quest started when some friends from church came to me with some information about a new local teen pageant. They were all going to compete, so they tried talking me into competing too. I remember telling my mom that I would *never* get into "that pageant stuff." But God had different plans. Isn't that the way it usually works?

Just three short years after that first pageant, I found myself getting ready to step onto the stage of Miss America. I'd worked hard to be prepared for every phase of competition, including the infamous swimsuit competition, which was the first night of preliminaries. Walking across the stage in high heels and wearing a bikini while five people judged me and millions watched is not my idea of fun. Getting into shape for that one evening took months of working with a personal trainer and diligently watching what food I consumed.

God smiled on me that night because I was awarded the overall swimsuit award. And to be totally honest, after that win I began to think I was hot stuff. I became obsessed with how I looked. I based my worth, my identity, and my potential success on my looks and what people thought about me.

As I've grown in my relationship with the Lord, I've realized how easy it is for girls and women to become focused on our outer appearance rather than on our inner beauty. We see magazines and television shows with glamorous, stick-thin models. We try so hard to measure up. But the truth is that all that is a mirage. The world has set unattainable, unrealistic goals for us when it comes to beauty. So if we base our worth on that, we will always be disappointed eventually.

What we see in the media has twisted our perception of what real beauty is. Do you buy into the lie that success is all about what you look like on the outside? God's Word tells a different story. In 1 Peter 3:3-4 it says, "Your beauty should not come from outward adornment, such as elaborate hairstyles and the wearing of gold jewelry or fine clothes. Rather, it should be that of your inner self, the unfading beauty of a gentle and quiet spirit, which is of great worth in God's sight."

We focus so much on outward beauty, but God's Word says true beauty doesn't consist of the right makeup, a trendy haircut, or wearing a certain size. God says your beauty comes from "your inner self." Your inner self is the Holy Spirit living inside you and working in your life for the world to see. The Bible says a spirit that is gentle and quiet is valuable to God. A woman with a gentle and quiet spirit is at peace. This peace comes from fully trusting in God and His purpose and plan for her life.

So how do we get there? How do we get to the point where we choose to see ourselves as God sees us instead of measuring ourselves against what the world says beauty or success is?

Some Truths About Pageant Life...

- Pageant girls use Firm Grip to keep swimsuit bottoms from riding up...just imagine girls spraying their behinds with Firm Grip and fanning and blowing on it till it dries. Quite an interesting sight!

- The rumor that pageant girls use Vaseline on their teeth to keep smiling...not true.

- Most pageant girls need help for an extra "oomph" on top. Some contestants use pads called "chicken cutlets."

- Contestants work out and eat right for months leading up to the swimsuit competition, but as soon as it is over, they can be seen backstage pigging out on candy, chips, and all kinds of junk food.

- There is a pageant myth that says you can tell who will win the contest before the big announcement. Look closely, when the final two girls are standing holding hands waiting for the winner's name to be read, the contestant who has her hand on top always wins. I'm not sure if this is scientifically proven, but it was true for me.

The only way to fight back against toxic thoughts is to fill your mind with God's truth about who you are and what He says about you. Psalm 45:11 says, "Let the king be enthralled by your beauty; honor him, for he is your lord." Did you catch it? Your focus is to please the King, and He will be *enthralled* by your beauty. That is good news, girl!

If we don't fill our hearts and minds with God's truth, the world and its lies can overtake us. Do you find yourself honing in on a critical remark a friend made about you? Do you replay in your mind something depressing you saw in a movie? God wants to preserve your thoughts and heart so that lies and hurts won't turn you away from the hope He offers. Proverbs 4:23 says, "Above all else, guard your heart, for everything you do flows from it." Protect your heart from believing the lies of this world by hiding His Word in your heart. Your heart is like a sponge by the kitchen sink. If you soak it in the dirty dishwater, that's what will rush out when it is squeezed. If your heart is soaked in God's truth, when you face trials, His truth will flow out of you.

The truth about physical beauty is that it can disappear just as quickly as it comes, and so do the titles and successes we hold so dearly. Miss America was one year out of my life. After 365 days, it was over. What I want you to know is that if we hold on to things such as our looks, our achievements, and our successes in life, we will always fall short of our potential in God. "Charm is deceptive, and beauty is fleeting; but a woman who fears the LORD is to be praised" (Proverbs 31:30). The only thing that lasts in this life is our relationship with God. I encourage you to find your worth in Him, not in temporary things.

A Bible Beauty Pageant

Did you know one of the very first beauty pageants is mentioned in the Bible? The prize for this pageant was not a college scholarship but marriage to a king. Grab your Bible and make your way to the book of Esther. We've put some key verses to the story in this chapter, but we encourage you to take some time to read Esther's amazing story. The book isn't very long, so read the entire thing when you get a chance.

Esther's road to royalty starts with the story of King Ahasuerus, also known as King Xerxes. He ruled over 127 provinces. He'd also conquered Israel. The king was married to Vashti. But after angering him, the queen lost her title and was banished, never to appear before the king again.

An all-out search began across the land for a new queen (Esther 2). All the young girls in the kingdom were brought to the palace, whether they wanted to be in the competition or not. Esther, whose Hebrew name was Hadassah, was one of those young women. Meeting the king meant having to go through "queen boot camp." Each young woman completed 12 months of beauty treatments. Talk about personal training! Not only did Esther receive a special diet, but she most likely was given new clothes, perfumes, and jewelry. Read the amazing facts in Esther!

When the king's order and edict had been proclaimed, many young women were brought to the citadel of Susa and put under the care of Hegai. Esther also was taken to the king's palace and entrusted to Hegai, who had charge of the harem. She pleased him and won his favor. Immediately he provided her with her beauty treatments and special food. He assigned to her seven female attendants selected from the king's palace and moved her and her attendants into the best place in the harem.

Esther had not revealed her nationality and family background, because Mordecai had forbidden her to do so. Every day he walked back and forth near the courtyard of the harem to find out how Esther was and what was happening to her.

Before a young woman's turn came to go in to King Xerxes, she had to complete twelve months of beauty treatments prescribed for the women, six months with oil of myrrh and six with perfumes and cosmetics. And this is how she would go to the king: Anything she wanted was given her to take with her from the harem to the king's palace. In the evening she would go there and in the morning return to another part of the harem to the care of Shaashgaz, the king's eunuch who was in charge of the concubines. She would not return to the king unless he was pleased with her and summoned her by name.

When the turn came for Esther (the young woman Mordecai had adopted, the daughter of his uncle Abihail) to go to the king, she asked for nothing other than what Hegai, the king's eunuch who was in charge of the harem, suggested. And Esther won the favor of everyone who saw her. She was taken to King Xerxes in the royal residence in the tenth month, the month of Tebeth, in the seventh year of his reign.

Now the king was attracted to Esther more than to any of the other women, and she won his favor and approval more than any of the other virgins. So he set a royal crown on her head and made her queen instead of Vashti. And the king gave a great banquet, Esther's banquet, for all his nobles and officials. He proclaimed a holiday throughout the provinces and distributed gifts with royal liberality (Esther 2:8-18).

Because God granted Esther favor, King Ahasuerus chose her as the new queen. In the midst of her selection, Scripture notes that the king was not aware of Esther's Jewish heritage. Soon after she was chosen, a plot by the evil Haman revealed a conspiracy to kill the Jews in the kingdom. For all of Esther's outer beauty treatments, her story reveals her greatest strength and beauty was found in her courage to risk death and reveal her identity to save her people.

God used a beauty pageant to save His people! In what circumstance can God use you? If you focus on who God wants you to be on the inside, He will use you to fulfill His purpose in many ways. For instance, did you collect Barbie dolls when you were younger? No matter whether you had Doctor Barbie, Veterinarian Barbie, or Astronaut Barbie, they all looked like Barbie. But the reality is that life doesn't parallel the Barbie world. God may call you into a number of special roles, but He created you unique and beautiful in His eyes. Learn today to see yourself in the mirror as the delightful girl God created you to be. He's crazy about you being you!

Personal Reflections

1. Use this simple exercise to help you view yourself as God does. Every time you look in the mirror, say out loud, "Thank You, God, that You see me as beautiful." Jot down how this changed your attitude about beauty.

2. Write down three things you don't like and three things you do like about your physical appearance. Which list is harder to come up with? Why do you think that is?

3. Describe internal beauty.

4. How can you develop your inner beauty?

5. Consider Lauren's example of the sponge. If you squeeze a sponge that has been soaking in dirty water, what will come out? What good things are you soaking in?

6. What traits in an individual's personality or relationship with God are attractive? How is this part of someone's beauty?

7. Have you been tempted to avoid eating to lose weight? Have you ever considered throwing up after eating to avoid the calories? If these are issues for you, please confide in your youth worker, small-group leader, a woman you trust, or your parents. Anorexia and bulimia are eating disorders that can scar you for life and even kill you. If you suspect you have a friend who has this problem, share your concerns with an adult you trust.

EVOLUTION OF DATING
WHAT HAPPENS NEXT?

Evolution: *A gradual process in which something changes into a different and usually more complex or better form; the process of gradual development.*

We've all been there. You meet a guy that you kind of like and ask yourself, "Now what?" It's the classic story. Girl meets boy. Girl likes boy. Girl wonders if boy likes her too. Have you been there? Relationships can be so confusing. And then there is the awkwardness of trying to define a relationship. Are you dating, just talking and hanging out, or just friends? What's a girl to do?

It's important to become the "right" girl before trying to find Mr. Right, but what happens when you find a guy you might be interested in while you're becoming the best you possible? We have learned from firsthand experience that it is easy to get things a little backward when it comes to the evolution of a relationship. Jumping in too soon or getting too serious too fast can lead to heartache and confusion for you and the guy.

from Lauren...
Moving Too Quickly

Relationships can get serious pretty quickly if we allow them. In fact, a little too serious. I can relate because it happened to me in high school. One moment things were pretty casual with my boyfriend, and the next minute he said, "I love you." I was totally caught off guard. I'd thought about what it might mean to tell him I loved him, but I definitely wasn't ready to say those words out loud. His three little words put me in a panic as soon as he blurted them out.

Not quite knowing how to respond, I came up with, "I like you a lot too." He looked at me like I was an alien from outer space. I'm sure it was pretty awkward for him because I know it was awkward for me. I explained that I wasn't ready to say those words yet. He was confused, but it didn't stop him from expressing his feelings now and then. It became normal for me to respond to his "I love you" with "I like you a lot too."

Time passed in our relationship, and I came to the point when I was ready to tell him that I loved him. But after I said "I love you," the relationship changed quickly. I jumped in with both feet. I allowed myself to get really close to him emotionally—even to the point of thinking he would be the guy I would one day marry. I remember writing "Lauren + Michael = Forever" on all my school notebooks. I really believed he was "the one."

Was he "the one"? No. But that relationship and those three little words taught me a great deal about the progression of relationships and how easy it is to move too quickly. It can lead you down a dangerous road emotionally, and put you in a position that leaves you vulnerable physically.

Enjoying Right Now

We grow up thinking about our Prince Charming. We dream of what our wedding will be like, the dress we will wear, and the man standing at the altar waiting for us. We get so engrossed in the thought of "someday" that we sometimes forget where we are living our "right now."

Your "right now" is a season of discovering a lot of new feelings and emotions regarding relationships with boys. You're not only changing physically, but you are evolving from the "boys have cooties" stage to the "boys are cuties" stage. Boys are getting taller, more muscular, and even beginning to grow facial hair. Ask any mom who has a daughter entering high school, and she'll secretly reveal her fear that the senior boys who share the same hallway as her freshman daughter aren't just little boys playing dodgeball at recess. They are young men with hormones.

This is a season of evolving. We're not talking about the "evolution of species" taught in science classes. We're talking about evolving from a girl to a young woman. The changes you are experiencing aren't just physical. They are also intellectual, emotional, and, most importantly, spiritual. One of the critical components in evolution is that it is a *gradual process*. It's not something that happens overnight but over a period of time. The result? You are becoming a different and more complex female.

One of the keys to enjoying "right now" is to not be in a hurry to move into serious relationships with guys. You will only be a teenager once. Try not to be in such a big hurry for your "someday" dreams that you forget to enjoy the blessings God has given you right now. We love this quote from cartoonist Bil Keane: "Yesterday is history, tomorrow is a mystery, but today is a gift. That's why it is called the present."

God knows you are moving into a new season of life, and He has not left you on your own to try to figure it out. In fact, He has a wonderful plan for your life and wants to direct each step. There are several Scriptures that refer to God's direction and plans. We offer some of our favorites and encourage you to memorize them over the next several weeks. Not sure how to do that? Pick out one (or more) of the verses, write them on a card, and tape them to your bathroom mirror and reflect on them during the day.

- *Psalm 84:11:* "For the Lord God is a sun and shield; the Lord bestows favor and honor; no good thing does he withhold from those whose walk is blameless."

- *Proverbs 3:5-6:* "Trust in the Lord with all your heart and lean not on your own understanding; in all your ways submit to him, and he will make your paths straight."

- *Proverbs 16:9:* "In their hearts humans plan their course, but the Lord establishes their steps."

- *Ecclesiastes 3:1:* "There is a time for everything, and a season for every activity under the heavens."

- *Jeremiah 29:11:* "'For I know the plans I have for you,' declares the Lord, 'plans to prosper you and not to harm you, plans to give you hope and a future.'"

- *Philippians 1:6:* "Being confident of this, that he who began a good work in you will carry it on to completion until the day of Christ Jesus."

God's plans are bigger than your own. His desire for your life is much more than you ever dream. And remember, God's plan is worked out in His timing, not yours. Following God doesn't mean life will always be perfect or without struggles. It just means God is the leader, the Lord of your life. And that includes the evolution of dating.

The Life Cycle of Dating

Just as every new life begins at conception, there is a beginning to the life cycle of relationships with guys. The fundamental relationship where dating should begin is not a new concept—just something you may have forgotten. It's called friendship.

It's easy to see a guy sitting on the other side of your math class and think, "Wow! He's so cute and amazing. He's the captain of the basketball team and is always around the popular people. I would love to be his girlfriend. If I could be his girlfriend, I would be the luckiest girl in the world."

But how well do you *really* know this guy? Do you know if he has a relationship with Christ? What's his family like? Does he treat his mom well? Do you have anything in common? Would he make you a better person or would he pull you down? Would he guard your emotional heart? Would maintaining physical purity be a priority for him?

Have you seen the movie *Thirteen Going on 30*? The story begins with Jenna, who desperately wants to be part of the "in" crowd. At her thirteenth birthday party, Jenna's geeky friend Matt makes her a dream dollhouse with "magic" dust. When deceived by her wannabe girlfriends in a game of "7 Minutes in Heaven," Jenna finds herself crying in the closet, and the magic dust from the dollhouse falls on her head. In a moment, Jenna is transported into the future. The awkward preteen becomes a gorgeous 30-year-old magazine editor who seems to have it all—the perfect job, popular friends, and a hockey-playing boyfriend.

The grown-up Jenna (who is still 13 in her mind) soon realizes the person she thought she wanted to be wasn't really that nice. She discovers the new Jenna is manipulating and deceiving. She tracks down her forgotten friend Matt, who is now engaged to someone else. Over time she realizes she missed out on the one guy who was not only her best friend but also the love she'd always dreamed of.

Never fear! With a little Hollywood magic, everything turns out wonderfully in the end (it always does in the best romantic comedies). Jenna finds true love based on a basic relationship principle—friendship.

We don't want to get too far ahead of ourselves because the next chapter is going to focus on the importance of guy friendships, but trust us on this one. Any great guy relationship should begin with friendship.

Just Talking

We sat down with some teen girls and asked them about the steps of dating. One of the first things we heard was the concept of "talking." When we asked girls if they were dating a guy, some of them responded, "We're not dating; we're just talking." But when we asked what "talking" was, we discovered it had a lot more to do with texting rather than having a voice conversation. Talking meant getting to know someone first through text messages.

That's really not so surprising. After all, we know how much teens love their phones and enjoy texting. In the fall of 2010, Nielsen ratings revealed that teenagers 13 to 17 send the most texts of any age group. The average teen sends 3,339 texts per month. The number for teen girls is even higher. Teen girls send an average of 4,050 texts per month, while boys send an average of 2,539 texts a month.[1]

from Robin...
"You Have Five Minutes"

The feeling of anticipation in my heart was overwhelming that day in the eighth grade. I remember it so clearly. My very first boyfriend asked if he could call me at home later that night. I waited anxiously right by the *only* phone we had, which was located near the kitchen. This was not a cordless phone I could take to my room. It was literally hooked to the wall with a long cord. The familiar sound of the ringing phone startled me. I darted to the old, gold-colored phone to make sure no one else in the family could answer it first. On the other end of the line was Ronnie. Nothing else around me mattered. My heart and my head were captivated by the sound of his voice. And he wanted to talk to me only!

In the midst of my excitement, I barely glanced at my dad, who was walking toward the kitchen stove. But then I heard something that got my attention—the sound of him setting the kitchen timer.

My dad was no dummy. He knew what was going on, and he knew who was on the other end of that phone call. As he walked by me again, he announced, "You have five minutes on the phone."

I was mortified. I was really bummed when the five minutes and my conversation with Mr. Wonderful had to end. Over time, we came up with a plan where Ronnie would call back several times so the five minutes would start several times during an evening.

Things sure have changed since my high school days! Today we live in a world of instant communication. There are some good things about that…and even some temptations. It's easy to turn your phone on silent and text without your parents' knowledge. And with that false sense of privacy and security from "listening ears," teens are just one button away from sending a picture or message that could damage their reputations and fill them with regret. I'm sure you understand what I'm talking about.

My dad's five-minute phone plan may seem outdated, but consider this: Would your private conversations sent through text messages be the same if your parents could instantly read every one? Do the messages you send honor God? Think about this carefully because this caution may help keep you from talking your way into trouble.

Friends Getting Together

If you've been "talking" to a guy (step 1) and the next step is in the future, we encourage you to get to know the guy better through a group setting. You might not even call it "group dating" because the time may just be a bunch of friends watching a movie or going to a school function together.

Whatever the activity may be, step 2 in the progression of dating is hanging out in a group. In these situations, you're able to observe your guy (and all the rest of them too) and see how he interacts with others. Groups give you opportunities to really see if this is a guy who will have your best interest at heart. One telltale sign is how he treats you in front of his friends. Group settings also protect you emotionally and physically because there are boundaries on behavior.

This stage of getting to know someone is also great for the guy. He can get to know you without the pressure of spending a lot of money or coming up with an evening of one-on-one conversation. Let's face it, most girls like to talk way more than most guys do. Groups are a relief for guys because they aren't expected to do a lot of talking.

If you're younger than 16, we suggest that this be the main way you hang out with guys. Depending on the guidelines given to you by your parents, most girls are wise to keep their relationships on a group level until they are ready to drive.

Being Exclusive

So you think you might be ready to go out with a guy one-on-one? Like we mentioned earlier, this step needs to be taken with your parents' approval. If you think you're ready to jump into a car with a guy and go to dinner and a movie, here are some questions you should be able to complete beforehand.

- How long have I known this guy?

- Have my parents met him? Do they approve of him?

- Has this guy spent time at my house with my family?

- Do I know the spiritual condition of this guy's heart? Is he someone who will help me grow spiritually?

- Has he talked to my father (or parental authority) and asked permission to take me out?

- Do we have a specific plan for the evening? Do I feel comfortable telling my parents what we're doing and when I'm going to be home? Will the guy help me stick to the plan?

- Will this guy honor and treat me with care and respect? Will he put me first, watch out for me, and even protect me if necessary?

- Do I trust him and his friends?

Depending on your age, these things will also evolve. If you're 16, don't proceed without making sure this is a guy you want to spend alone time with. When you get older, there are going to be hurdles to overcome regarding how well your parents will know the guys you date, especially if you go to college in a different state. But no matter how old you are, jumping into one-on-one dating is a big step in any relationship.

Getting Your Parents Onboard

We want to emphasize how important it is to discuss and work out your dating progression plans with your parents. Their guidance, rules, and awareness are crucial for your positive, healthy, safe development from a growing girl to a dating young woman.

The commandment "Honor your father and your mother" is not just an Old Testament standard (Exodus 20:12). God is pleased when you submit to the authority of your parents. Believe it or not, they have walked the steps you're walking and can be a great source of wisdom. They know a lot more about dating and relationships than your friends at school. And if you don't have a parent you can go to, find a youth worker or a trusted adult at church who is willing to help you navigate the world of dating.

Can You Go Back?

You might be thinking, "I've jumped way ahead in this process, and I'd like to go back to a less-involved time." Is that possible? Yes, but it will take effort and commitment!

Maybe you've already been on a one-on-one date with a guy, and you noticed some red flags or concerns. There's nothing wrong with taking a step back and being honest about your feelings. Explain to the guy that you'd like to spend more time hanging out with him in a group setting or that you need a break for a while. Be mindful that guys have feelings too. Treat them the same way you want to be treated.

When Dating Ends

Let's face it. You are most likely going to date several guys before meeting Mr. Right. So what does that mean? That some of the relationships that begin will probably come to an end. (The alternative is marriage.)

Coming to the end of a relationship is difficult. While you might desire to maintain a friendship with the guy, don't be surprised if he's not willing to return to just being your buddy. Depending on who ends the relationship and how it ended, there might be some awkwardness you'll need to work through. This can be especially difficult if you have the same circle of friends. Honor the friendship, and be extremely careful about the words you say and text. The book of Proverbs has many verses about the power of words. We especially like Proverbs 16:24: "Gracious words are a honeycomb, sweet to the soul and healing to the bones." Your words can still be kind after a breakup, and they should bring healing to the relationship.

Before ending a relationship, think about the words you'll use. They may very well leave a lasting impression on the other person. Be sure you aren't being hurtful in what you say or do. Also, don't play mind games by flirting with the guy after you break up. This is one of the most crucial points when a relationship ends. Far too often a girl ends a relationship with a guy, and within a week she's having doubts and second-guessing her decision. (This can also happen when the guy ends the relationship.) It's easy to keep sending text messages and checking on the other person. Why? Because you've developed a friendship, and you're accustomed to communicating on a regular basis. Depending on how the relationship ends, sometimes it's okay to keep the communication line open. But if you really want to end the relationship, you may need to give the other person space to work through what happened.

The danger of ending a relationship and continuing to communicate is that it can send a "mixed signal." Thoughts like "Does he still like me?" or "Maybe we'll get back together" can be very natural, depending on the intensity of your relationship. This can be even trickier when your "former" boyfriend starts liking someone else. If you begin to sense the monster called envy taking over your thoughts, examine your motives and attitude.

What can you do when the relationship ends so you still retain some form of a friendship? To be honest, sometimes it just doesn't happen. While it would be wonderful to transition from boyfriend/girlfriend back to "just friends," sometimes moving back to the friendship stage can take a long time. This can be even more difficult if you attend the same school or church. While every situation is different, here are some helpful hints for this awkward stage.

Acknowledge the person. If you've ended the relationship and you'll still be seeing each other in math class every day, take the time to say hello. Ask how he is doing. It's not going to be easy, but it's a first step. Few things are more hurtful than pretending a person doesn't exist.

Look for group situations where others will provide conversation. It's much easier to be around your "former" when you're surrounded by friends. Find activities to reconnect with your friends or seek new opportunities to make new friends. Use this time to enjoy the freedom of not being in a relationship.

Time is your friend. It may take weeks or even longer for you to be comfortable around someone you used to like. Just like a bad scrape on your knee, it takes time to heal. But eventually the hurt will. You may even be left with some scars, but trust us. There will eventually be a day when you don't feel the pain.

Am I Weird If I'm Not Dating?

So you're a senior in high school. You've never had a date, and you've never been kissed. Is something wrong with you? Absolutely not! There are many young people who go through high school (and even college) without dating. You're not an alien, and you aren't weird. What is weird about saving yourself for later? The Lord would much rather you wait on His timing than compromise your standards for a guy who doesn't honor Him or isn't the best person for you.

We've heard some girls say, "I don't want to go to college without ever being kissed!" We get it. You want to experience that level of physical intimacy. But save your kisses for the right guy. You'll never regret it.

What Does the Bible Say About Dating?

The Bible doesn't have a step-by-step plan for dating, but God's Word does give us some standards for the types of guys His girls should be attracted to. We know God's Word instructs us to remain sexually pure before marriage. And we know dating unbelievers is off-limits: "Do not be yoked together with unbelievers. For what do righteousness and wickedness have in common? Or what fellowship can light have with darkness?" (2 Corinthians 6:14).

So why isn't dating discussed in the Bible? Before 1900, most soon-to-be couples were introduced to each other through religious activities (such as church) or through families. One big invention changed this—the automobile. The car gave young people more freedom to go places without chaperones. Soon parental authority was replaced by peer influence.

So you won't find a lot of dating stories in the Bible. But you will discover a lot of stories about courtship, love, and marriage.

A Biblical Yet Modern Romance

If the book of Ruth were to be portrayed in a contemporary film, it would probably rank as one of the best romance stories told. There is high drama, complete with unexpected death, unexpected romance, and a happily ever after ending. It is God's "chick flick" to humanity.

Suffice it to say, we could spend pages upon pages sharing the story of Ruth and Boaz. Instead, we encourage you to stop reading right now, open your Bible, and read the entire book just as you would a novel. There are only four chapters, and you can easily finish it in a short time. After you finish, come back and we'll share some important highlights and how they will help you with guys.

Ruth, Chapter 1

The opening of the book gives us Ruth's background. She was a Moabite woman who married an Israelite. Moabites were despised by Israelites because they were known for following pagan gods. At some point, Ruth discovers the one true God, perhaps after she marries Naomi's son. Then tragedy strikes. The man she marries dies, and she must go back to her Moabite family or follow her mother-in-law (who is also widowed) to Bethlehem. Ruth chooses to go with Naomi: "Don't urge me to leave you or to turn back from you. Where you go I will go, and where you stay I will stay. Your people will be my people and your God my God. Where you die I will die, and there I will be buried. May the LORD deal with me, be it ever so severely, if even death separates you and me" (Ruth 1:16-18).

The take-away: The first and most important relationship in your life should be with God. Loyalty to Him should be the top priority in any guy/girl relationship.

Ruth, Chapter 2

Through a series of God-ordained events, Ruth knows who Boaz is—a wealthy landowner—because she gleans wheat in his field. This practice was allowed to help people who were in need of food. Boaz notices Ruth, inquires about her, takes an interest in her welfare, and shows great compassion. He protects her physically, he provides abundantly, and he even guards her emotionally. The sparks of relationship fly.

The take-away: Ruth didn't approach Boaz. He noticed her and pursued getting to know her. Allow guys the chance to pursue you. Boaz was a guy Ruth could trust because she knew he had her best interest in mind by his actions. Guys who value you above their own desires are worth hanging on to. Look for selfless young men who will honor and protect you.

Ruth, Chapter 3

Naomi devises a plan that would be rated PG-13 for most of us. She instructs Ruth to make her move by lying down next to Boaz one evening while he is asleep. When Boaz notices her, Ruth explains her need for a guardian-redeemer (or kinsman-redeemer)—someone who will take care of her family and provide for her. Again, Boaz reveals his godly character. He treats her with respect, protects her reputation, and sets out to get the permission he needs to marry Ruth.

The take-away: We're not advocating the tactics of Naomi, but we do like that Boaz shows his protective side. He is most concerned about Ruth's welfare and character. Choose guys who won't tarnish your character. You want a guy who will make your character shine to the world.

Ruth, Chapter 4

Boaz makes arrangements to properly marry Ruth. It is a happy ending to their romance, but the greater ending happens much later. After they married, their offspring included David, who would become king of Israel. And their family lineage includes Jesus Christ! "Boaz the father of Obed, whose mother was Ruth, Obed the father of Jesse, and Jesse the father of King David…And Jacob the father of Joseph, the husband of Mary, and Mary was the mother of Jesus who is called the Messiah" (Matthew 1:5-6,16).

The take-away: Leave the results of your relationships to God. Understand Isaiah 55:8, "'My thoughts are not your thoughts, neither are your ways my ways,' declares the LORD." God knows your future, and you can place your trust in Him.

This has been a preview of the book of Ruth and the evolution of their relationship. But what an ending! Because Ruth and Boaz had a God-honoring relationship, you and I are blessed through the birth, death, and resurrection of Christ! You can trust God with the progression of your relationships, especially when you understand His plan is bigger and better than what you can imagine and extends far beyond you, even into the generations that will follow.

Personal Reflections

1. Look back at Lauren's story of moving too quickly in a relationship. Has that ever happened to you? How did you handle that situation?

2. Have you talked to your parents about guy relationships and dating? Do you know their expectations and guidelines? Write about those guidelines and how you can guard your heart by following them.

3. Are you "talking" to a guy by texting? Do your conversations honor God? Would you be embarrassed if others saw or knew what you share with this guy? If yes, does this raise a red flag for you?

4. How can you be accountable to others regarding your guy communications?

5. Look through the verses listed under "Enjoying Right Now." Pick one or two to memorize over the next few weeks. Write down which ones they are in the space below. If you're reading this book as part of a group, plan to share the verses from memory at the next meeting. If you're doing this study on your own, share the verses with a friend or your parents.

6. Look through the book of Ruth. There are so many gems in this story! Describe what you learned through Ruth's experiences.

7. Look up the following verses, answer the questions, and discuss them in your small group or with a friend.

   • *Ruth 1:1:* What do you discover about Bethlehem? Why did Elimelech and Naomi move away?

   • *Ruth 1:16:* Why do you think Ruth was so convicted to go back to Bethlehem with Naomi? What does this tell you about Ruth's relationship with Naomi and with God?

   • *Ruth 2:1:* What do you think it means when Boaz is described as a "man of standing"?

   • *Ruth 2:9:* What does Boaz's instruction say about the way he protected her physically?

   • *Ruth 2:15:* How does Boaz protect Ruth emotionally?

- *Ruth 2:22:* What does this verse say about who people should hang out with?

- *Ruth 3:11:* What does this verse say about Ruth's character? Why do you think Ruth has this reputation?

- *Ruth 4:14-17:* What do these verses say about God's plan for Ruth?

8. Why can you trust God with your future relationships? How will you do that?

BOY FRIENDS AND BOYFRIENDS

WHAT'S THE DIFFERENCE?

Friend: *a person attached to another by feelings of affection or personal regard; a person who is on good terms with another; a person who is not hostile.*

The words "boy friend" and "boyfriend" may sound alike, but there's a huge gap in the middle—literally and figuratively. Having guy friends is a great thing, but girls have to be really careful about the signals they send. If you're not, your innocent playfulness toward guys may be misinterpreted.

from Lauren...
When the Friendship Line Blurs

In high school I had a group of friends who did everything together. There were five of us—two girls and three guys. We were inseparable. In fact, inseparable might be an understatement. We went to games together. We took prom pictures together. We were in Show Choir together. We did almost everything together. Get the picture?

But somewhere in the midst of our great friendship, the lines got a little blurry. None of us had ever dated each other, and I thought we were all just a big group of friends. Boy, was I wrong.

One day before math, one of the "Fab Five" guys passed me a note. I was blown away when I read it. My guy friend told me he had feelings for me beyond just friendship. He thought I'd given him a reason to believe I was interested in him in a special way. He told me I must like him because of the way I'd been flirting. Talk about a sticky situation!

Having a guy friend was really important to me. I liked having a guy I trusted and could ask for advice. Now I realized he had interpreted that as meaning more than I intended. In a sense I was leading him on, even though I didn't know it. The line of friendship had blurred.

What did I do? I was honest. I told him our relationship was on a friendship level and nothing more. It was a tough conversation because I didn't want to hurt his feelings or let him think I didn't care about him.

I wish I had been a lot clearer in my communication with him before he gave me the note. I wish I'd known to set some boundaries long before that time so we could have avoided that awkward conversation.

What Are You Looking For?

So what are the differences between friends who are boys and boyfriends? The next few pages are going to be a little different. Don't jump ahead! Take the time to really think through this simple exercise on friendship.

Friend Qualities You Look For

Funny	Physically attractive	Active in church
Smart	Good listener	and missions
Godly	Likes animals	Loyal
Athletic	Enjoys the outdoors	Honest
Likes to shop	Holds you	Plays a musical
Accepting	accountable	instrument
Enjoys movies	Likes to read	Compassionate
Likes the same music	Has the same values	toward others
Encouraging	Wise	Likes games
Enjoys video games	Family is important	

Using the list of "Friend Qualities You Look For" and other adjectives you come up with, grab a pen and on the next page list the characteristics you look for in a girlfriend.

Then list the qualities and characteristics you look for in a guy friend.

Now list the qualities and characteristics you look for in a boyfriend.

Go ahead and take some time to do this. We're sure you'll find it very revealing about what you really want, hope for, and expect in relationships. This will also remind you of the qualities you want to possess so you will be a good friend.

Girlfriends

List at least 5 things you look for in a girlfriend.

-
-
-
-
-

Boy Friends

List at least 5 things you look for in a guy friend.

-
-
-
-
-

Boyfriend

List at least 5 things you look for in a boyfriend.

-
-
-
-
-

Once you've completed that fun little assignment, look over each list. Then:

- Circle the words or qualities that are alike on at least two of the lists. (For instance, you might have listed "good listener" under all three sections.)

- Put a star by the quality on each list that seems the most unique to that list. (For instance, you might have written "physically attractive" on the boyfriend list and not on the other lists.)

Consider these questions and take a moment to write down your answers.

- Why might there be a big difference between the boy friend list and the boyfriend list?

- What do girlfriends offer in friendships that guys usually don't?

- Do you think you should date your guy friends? Why or why not?

You Were Made for Friendship

All of us were born needy. We all need God in our lives. We all need people in our lives. And life would be pretty boring if we didn't have a wide variety of friendships. Each person God brings into our lives offers something unique and different. You might have some friends who are your shopping friends, and they may not be the same people you would go to a basketball game with. You might have one friend who enjoys the same music you do, and yet another friend you choose to exercise with. The best thing about friendships is they are rich and varied because God makes everyone special. We can learn and appreciate new and different things as our friendships expand to include guys.

Having good guy friends during this time in your life is extremely important because someday we hope you will marry your best friend! We hope that you'll find a guy who makes your heart flutter, who is someone you can talk to and confide in, and who is someone you enjoy sharing activities with. Some of the best marriages we've seen are strong because the couples love being together.

Another reason why you should be developing guy friends is that you'll learn what you like and dislike about certain guys. Do you enjoy being around guys who make you laugh? Or maybe you have a guy friend who is a little too clingy, and you realize how uncomfortable that makes you feel. Do you have guy friends who like you no matter what you look like? Spending a lot of time with someone allows both of you to evaluate if the friendship or relationship is complementary. While spending time together invariably reveals differences in opinions, attitudes, and beliefs, remember that core values remain constant.

The Bible has some helpful verses about the qualities to look for in all three types of relationships—girlfriend, guy friend, and boyfriend. Here are a few examples of character traits God outlines as priorities.

Honesty. Proverbs 27:6 says, "Wounds from a friend can be trusted, but an enemy multiplies kisses." Sometimes friends may have to tell you things that are hard to hear, but a true friend will be honest. The friends you can't trust are those who offer flattery instead of honesty.

Accountability. Proverbs 27:17 says, "As iron sharpens iron, so one person sharpens another." Hang out with friends who make you better socially, academically, physically, and spiritually.

Loyalty. First Samuel 18:1 says, "Jonathan became one in spirit with David, and he loved him as himself." These two guy friends had remarkable loyalty toward each other. When Jonathan's father, King Saul, threatened David's life, Jonathan protected his friend. Even after Jonathan died, David honored his memory. David asked, "Is there anyone still left of the house of Saul to whom I can show kindness for Jonathan's sake?" (2 Samuel 9:1).

Encouragement. There's nothing worse than having a friend who talks poorly about you to others when you leave the room. Proverbs 16:28 says, "A perverse person stirs up conflict, and a gossip separates close friends." Distance yourself from those who cut you down around others. Instead, look for friends who will build you up.

Wisdom. All of us need friends we can go to when we need advice. Remember to pick friends and mentors who will give you godly wisdom, not the latest advice from a TV show or famous personality. Proverbs 27:9 says, "The pleasantness of a friend springs from their heartfelt advice."

Were any of these characteristics on your original lists of qualities you look for in a friend? If not, do you think you should add them to all three categories?

from Lauren...

Should You Date Your Guy Friend?

From sixth grade until my senior year of high school, I lived next door to the guy every girl wanted to date. Whether he was playing quarterback on the football team or playing on the baseball team, he was an all-around, all-star athlete. He became known as "cutie pie" in my house, and my little sister would spy on him from our bedroom window. Needless to say, he was a heartthrob. He was also a really good friend. We navigated the awkwardness of middle school, and although he dated someone else, I always had a little crush on him.

During the last semester of high school, he broke up with his girlfriend. Everyone at school knew because it was the hottest topic in the gossip circles. I had also ended a relationship around that time, so "cutie pie" and I found ourselves single and without a date to the prom.

When he asked me to go to the dance with him, I couldn't turn him down. What girl would say no to the school heartthrob? We soon started dating, but it didn't take me long to discover he was a better boy friend than boyfriend. It wasn't that he did anything wrong, I just knew we were better at being friends and next-door neighbors than being a couple.

The saddest part is that our friendship never was the same again. Not only did I lose a boyfriend, but I lost a good guy friend when we broke up.

I realize there are certain friendships that may evolve into a dating relationship. We saw that in the last chapter when we talked about the evolution of dating. But in this personal situation, I realized that we made the next step only because it was convenient and solved an immediate problem—a date to the prom. I realized that certain friendships should remain exactly that—friendships.

So when you're trying to figure out where you stand with a guy friend, remember that the transition from boy friend to boyfriend isn't necessarily the right progression for that relationship. Don't lose a great friend because you're trying to make the connection you have something it isn't meant to be.

Friends with Benefits?

Just as there are positive characteristics you should look for in guy friendships, there are definitely red flags to be on the lookout for too. You've heard the phrase "friends with benefits," and maybe you've even seen the movie. There's a growing trend among guys and girls to use each other for physical intimacy and believe there can be "no strings attached" regarding other aspects of their relationship. Whether it's kissing or sex, basing friendships on or abusing friendships for physical pleasure is playing with fire. And, girl, you will *always* get burned. There is no such thing as physical intimacy without emotional attachment, especially for girls and women.

The Bible has some pretty serious words about "friends with benefits." First Thessalonians 4:3-6 says:

> It is God's will that you should be sanctified: that you should avoid sexual immorality; that each of you should learn to control your own body in a way that is holy and honorable, not in passionate lust like the pagans, who do not know God; and that in this matter no one should wrong or take advantage of a brother or sister. The Lord will punish all those who commit such sins.

One commentary cited on bibletools.org labels this action as cheating:

> The essence of what Paul is saying here is that even before a man is married, he can cheat his future spouse out of something! A man can be cheated out of the experience of completely sharing himself with a woman, who is in turn completely sharing herself with him, in a way neither of them has experienced before. Even if a man is not yet married, in essence he already "belongs" to the woman that he will eventually marry, and vice versa for the woman. Even when not married, we have to conduct ourselves as though we are![1]

Why Have Guy Friends?

Chad Eastham, a popular speaker and author, explains the importance of friendships in his book *The Truth About Dating, Love and Just Being Friends*. He says, "We aren't longing for boyfriends or girlfriends. We are longing to be known, to be loved and to feel significant. And 'just' being a friend is actually a pretty great place to start. There is no 'just' in real friendship."[2]

Having healthy guy friendships is essential to healthy development during your teen years. Why? You're going to be surrounded by the male gender for the rest of your life. Right now you are developing friendships with guys in your church youth group, at school, and through your extracurricular activities. As you get older, you'll most likely be in a work environment with men and women. And while it's hard to think about this right now, you may someday be a mom—and you just might be raising a boy. Consider Robin's take as a mom.

from Robin...
A Mom's Perspective

There's a pretty personal reason behind the writing of this book—a special blessing God placed in my life. This blessing is the reason I have a burden for you and other girls your age. The blessing is a special young man in my life—my son, Cade.

I know how important it is for Cade to grow and become a godly man. I pray for him every day. One of my most earnest prayers is regarding the friends he chooses right now. This includes the guys he plays football with as well as the girls at his school. Why? Because I know there will be a day when Cade will want to date a girl, and I want that relationship to honor God.

For a moment, I want you to think about the boy/mom relationship. There's something unique about it. I've been the first "girl" in his life. I've been the first girl to hold his hand and wipe away his tears. I'm the first girl to show him respect and unconditional love.

I know it won't be long before Cade grows up and becomes a man. There will be a point when another girl will capture his heart. That's exciting! My prayer is that Cade will discover a young woman who loves

God with all her heart, who understands the importance of putting God first, and who will be committed to the words at the end of the traditional marriage vow: "so help me God."

I will never be replaced as Cade's mom, but when the time is right, it will be a blessing to step aside and watch a new woman walk by his side—a woman who honors God with her life and loves my son.

Personal Reflections

♥ ♥ ♥

1. How has this chapter changed what you look for in a boyfriend?

2. How can you be a better friend?

3. Are you blurring the lines between boy friend and boyfriend? If yes, what behaviors will you change?

4. Think of someone in your life who builds you up. Share about that person.

   My friend builds me up by…

   My friend helps me grow closer to God by…

   I appreciate the way my friend…

   I admire these strengths in my friend…

   My friend is fun to be around because…

   When I spend time with my friend, he or she makes me feel…

5. What can you do to build up your friends? How will you encourage your friends this week?

FINDING MR. RIGHT
INSTEAD OF LOOKING FOR MR. PERFECT

Perfect: *Without errors, flaws, or fault; complete and lacking nothing; excellent or ideal in every way.*

It's time to use your imagination and dream a little. Consider for a moment what the perfect prom night might be like for you.

The Perfect Prom Date

My perfect prom date will be with...

The perfect way my date will ask me to the prom is...

My perfect prom dress will be...

The perfect flowers my date will bring me are...

The perfect car to go to the prom in will be...

The perfect "before prom" meal will be...

The perfect prom dance and song will be...

The perfect prom pictures will be taken at (time and location)...

The perfect after-prom activity will include...

The perfect ending to my prom date will be...

Is it wrong to dream about the perfect prom date? What about the perfect mate? The problem is that "Mr. Perfect" is not the same as "Mr. Right." And because boys tend to take longer to mature in many ways, you might not recognize or discover Mr. Right for several years.

The Dating Mystery

Let's go back in time—all the way back to 1965. Yep, back before man walked on the moon and microwave ovens were commonplace. Although it might seem like the dark ages way back then, we want to introduce you to one of the most popular board games of that decade: "Mystery Date." An updated version of the game even came out years later featuring the stars from the movie *High School Musical*.

The object of "Mystery Date" was to acquire three cards that would complete a matching outfit. Then you could open the "front door" feature on the board. When you opened the door, your date was revealed. The handsome, well-built man would either be dressed up for a formal dance date, a beach date, a ski date, or a bowling date. The date you hoped to avoid was the skinny, nerdy guy. (We're not dismissing nerdy guys. This game was all about appearances.) Just for fun, go to YouTube and watch the 1960 commercial for the game. It's hilarious!

"Mystery Date" sure didn't do any favors for guys. It was one more way unrealistic expectations were put on them. It also affected the way girls looked at boys, concentrating on outer appearance rather than looking at their hearts and character. Let's just say "Mystery Date" was shallow.

The reality of dating is more like one of the scenes from the movie *The Princess Diaries*. Mia dreams of her perfect date with Josh, the popular boy at school. She wishes for a wonderful kiss to end her perfect evening. Her dream date turned out to be more of a dud when Josh revealed his selfish side and desire for fame. Mia's expectation of a foot-popping kiss turned into getting her foot caught in a fishing net. Her unrealistic expectations quickly faded, a frequent occurrence in real life, we've found.

Let's be really clear. We're not saying you should have low expectations for guys or settle for someone who doesn't meet God's standards. You are precious, and you deserve someone who will cherish you. But instead of spending all your time making a list of the perfect guy, please understand that God is more interested in who you are becoming than who you are dating.

from Lauren...

My Mr. Right Is Not a Jesus Substitute

God has really blessed me with an incredible husband. Randy is everything a woman would want. He's kind, funny, compassionate, intelligent, and crazy about Jesus. By the way, he's also really handsome! He plays guitar, and we lead worship together each week at our church. Randy is a "great catch"!

Although Randy possesses wonderful qualities, he still can't fill the place in my heart that belongs to Christ. My husband is human, and so am I. That means we're going to make mistakes. There are times when we let each other down or hurt each other's feelings. Most important, Randy is the spiritual leader in our relationship, but he's not my Holy Spirit substitute.

I really urge you to make the Lord your top priority and place other relationships after Him. I still remember when Randy explained this to me when we were dating. He said he loved Jesus more than he loved me. I have to admit, that statement seemed a little odd at first and hard to take. But as my spiritual walk deepened, I began to understand what Randy meant. I've realized that the more I love Christ, the more I can love my husband.

Where Is Mr. Righteous?

Longing to meet and know a guy who is righteous is a good thing, but first, do you know what righteousness looks like? The Bible says, "There is no one righteous, not even one" (Romans 3:10). Isaiah 64:6 affirms this: "All of us have become like one who is unclean, and all our righteous acts are like filthy rags." In simple terms, no one is "right" before God. To be righteous on God's terms, a person would have to be innocent, holy, and without sin.

None of us is righteous on our own. But because Christ came and took our sin on Himself and paid the price we owed, we have the opportunity to stand "right" before God. When we accept Christ as our personal Savior, we obtain righteousness through Him. Being right before God will also help you recognize righteousness in others, including guys.

There are a couple of difficult words to describe what Christ has done for us. These words and their meanings can get a little deep, so hang in here with us. We're not trying to make this complicated, but we really want you to grab hold of these concepts.

Justification. The easiest way to explain justification is to think about someone who is on trial and standing before a judge. The person on trial is guilty, and the judge knows it. Out of the blue, another person enters the courtroom, approaches the bench, and asks the judge if he can take the punishment for the guilty criminal. Now imagine you are the guilty person on trial. In fact, this isn't something you have to imagine, because it's real. You are guilty because everyone has sinned against God (Romans 3:23). But guess what? There was Someone who came and took your punishment, and His name is Jesus.

Christ died for your sins and the sins of everyone. He took your well-deserved guilty verdict on Himself and declared you to be innocent. That's what Christianity terms "justification." The apostle Paul said, "God made him who had no sin to be sin for us, so that in him we might become the righteousness of God" (2 Corinthians 5:21). Your salvation through faith in Christ makes you "right" or "righteous" before God.

Sanctification. Stay with us because this is a biggie. "Sanctification" means "to be set apart" or "to be holy." This is a *continual* process that only occurs because the Holy Spirit lives within you. It is the process of God conforming you to His image each day.

Let's say you are learning what it means to serve others. Because serving others is a characteristic of God, the more you serve, the more you become like Christ. Got it? Here's another way to think about it. Let's say you are at church, and you learn something from God's Word. When you apply what you learned and it becomes part of your life, you are being sanctified, you are becoming more like Christ. Romans 12:1-2 says, "Offer your bodies as a living sacrifice, holy and pleasing to God—this is your true and proper worship. Do not conform to the pattern of this world, but be transformed by the renewing of your mind."

"Justification" and "sanctification" can be boiled down to a simple principle when it comes to finding Mr. Right. The first quality you want in a guy is righteousness.

from Lauren...
The Wrong Path of "Mr. Right Now"

During my time as Miss America, I found myself relying on a "Mr. Right Now." We'd started dating a few months after I was crowned Miss Oklahoma, and the relationship continued through 2007, the year I was Miss America.

In the role of Miss America, I traveled all the time. During those 12 months, I covered approximately 240,000 miles. I was away from my family almost every day. I was surrounded by people, yet I was desperately lonely. Because of this, I started relying on my boyfriend to fill the loneliness. He was the one consistent presence in my life, other than my immediate family. I placed a lot of importance on him, and I relied on him to fill my emptiness. But it didn't work.

I now understand that only God is able to fill that emptiness. Have you felt that way? You may try to fill the emptiness with possessions, approval, and relationships, but those never last. I discovered the truth of 2 Corinthians 12:9, where Paul writes that Jesus said to him, "My grace is sufficient for you, for my power is made perfect in weakness." "Sufficient" means that God is enough for the purpose. God's grace is enough for me, and it's enough for you. I love the attitude offered in Psalm 73:25: "Whom have I in heaven but you [oh Lord]? And earth has nothing I desire besides you." When all is said and done, nothing is as important or as worthy of our affection and desire as Christ and His love.

What to Include on Your "Mr. Right" List

Remember the list you made of what you're looking for in a boyfriend? Before that, did you ever make a list of your dream guy's qualities? We want to give you a few more things to consider when you're contemplating life and love.

Your personal walk with God. That's right. Your list should first concentrate on you becoming the young woman God designed you to be. Jesus said, "Blessed are those who hunger and thirst for righteousness, for they will be filled" (Matthew 5:6). How can you expect to attract a godly guy if you're not working each day to be more like Christ? So make your spiritual walk your top priority. Get in God's Word. Have a consistent quiet time with the Lord. Ask God to help you have a heart that desires to be more like His Son each day.

A guy who loves the Lord first. Luke 10:27 says, "Love the Lord your God with all your heart and with all your soul and with all your strength and with all your mind." Not only should you be making Christ a priority, but you should consider only dating guys who also put God first.

Someone who is considerate and compassionate toward others. Philippians 2:3-4 says, "Do nothing out of selfish ambition or vain conceit. Rather, in humility value others above yourselves, not looking to your own interests but each of you to the interests of others." If you date a guy who knows how to love others, he's a pretty good catch. Also note how he treats his mom, his dad, his friends, his teachers, and people at church. Actions speak louder than words.

Someone who will challenge you to become spiritually stronger. Hebrews 10:24 says, "Let us consider how we may spur one another on toward love and good deeds." Just as you need girlfriends who will challenge you to be more like Christ, only consider dating a guy who encourages you in your faith. This doesn't mean you have to find a guy who has the Bible memorized, but you do want to date someone who seriously desires to *grow* in his walk with the Lord.

Things Not to Have on Your List

Outward appearance. When Samuel was looking for the person God had chosen to be Israel's future king, God told him, "The LORD does not look at the things people look at. People look at the outward appearance, but the LORD looks at the heart" (1 Samuel 16:7). If your list includes how tall your dream guy is and what color his eyes are, you will probably be disappointed during the dating process. It's okay if you like guys who are tall and muscular, but those things tend to disappear with time. Just ask your dad or look at photos of him as a teenager. We're sure he no longer looks like he did back then.

Future career plans. "Commit your actions to the LORD, and your plans will succeed" (Proverbs 16:3 NLT). Do you have an expectation that you are going to marry a doctor? What about someone in ministry? Those ideas are good, but if you limit yourself to only dating guys who are heading down a certain career path, you will probably be disappointed. Trust God with your future—what He has planned for your life and the life of your future spouse. If you feel called to ministry, pray God will lead you to someone with a similar calling. Be open to how God will fulfill that calling.

Future riches. Do you believe material wealth will bring happiness? Proverbs 11:28 says, "Those who trust in their riches will fall, but the righteous will thrive like a green leaf." Don't judge guys on the things they have or how much money they might make. Focus more on whether the guy you like is generous with what he has.

Faithfulness of a Man, Faithfulness of God

Tucked away in the Old Testament is the incredible love story of a prophet who was loyal to his wife even in the midst of betrayal. It's the story of Hosea and Gomer. Hosea was devoted to serving God. Most likely he had a high standard for the type of woman he would marry. Instead, God instructed him to marry Gomer, a prostitute:

> When the LORD first began speaking to Israel through Hosea, he said to him, "Go and marry a prostitute, so that some of her children will be conceived in prostitution. This will illustrate how Israel has acted like a prostitute by turning against the LORD and worshiping other gods" (Hosea 1:2 NLT).

It's safe to say that a prostitute wasn't on Hosea's list for Mrs. Right. Despite this strange and shocking command, Hosea trusted God and did as He asked. So Hosea married Gomer. And even though she was unfaithful, he continued to pursue her and love her despite her sin.

This story is not only a picture of one man's faithfulness to his wife, but a picture of God's faithfulness to you and me. Hosea's marriage shows his unfailing love, but it also shows God's unfailing love. God chooses to forgive, just as Hosea forgave Gomer. Hosea 3:1 says, "The LORD said to [Hosea], 'Go, show your love to your wife again, though she is loved by another man and is an adulteress. Love her as the LORD loves the Israelites.'"

What can we learn from this Mr. Right who married the less-than-perfect Mrs. Right? God can take our mistakes, even when we're far from perfect and unfaithful, and use them for His eternal purposes.

from Robin...
When Plans Fail

Dating is difficult no matter how young or old you might be. I discovered this the hard way when I became single again a few years ago. After being married for nine years, serving in ministry with my spouse, and having a beautiful baby boy, I found myself in frightening territory. Within a few months, I was divorced. This was definitely not in my life plan. My "perfect world" came crashing down in the blink of an eye. I was heartbroken and devastated, and I lived in fear of never finding love again. I was desperate for God to guide me and show me how to be a single mom and to carry on with life.

Thankfully, the Lord knew my sorrow, and He was faithful. During the darkest time in my life, God gave me a lifeline—His Word. I began to keep a journal. I learned to give thanks in all things, even when it was hard to be grateful. I wrote down the ways God continued to bless me. I wrote down the ways God showed me how to take steps forward even when I felt like life was tumbling backward.

Several months later, I prayed about the possibility of dating again. I'd been thinking about the story of Ruth and Boaz. In my attempt to find humor in the situation, I wrote in my journal, "Don't date a bunch of bozos to get to a Boaz." God impressed on me that I shouldn't waste my time on relationships with guys who weren't committed to Him. Waiting for Mr. Right was much easier knowing that God's way would be better than my own.

And God was faithful in His promise! I met Keith, my own "Boaz." We've celebrated several years of marriage now, and our "chance" meeting was truly a God thing. (I can't wait to tell you more about Keith, which I'll do in chapter 7.)

Take the Pledge

It's your turn. Are you ready to commit to finding Mr. Right and not Mr. Perfect? We know there are lots of ways you can commit your dating life to the Lord. Purity rings and ceremonies are wonderful ways to take a stand and say, "I'm waiting for God's best in my life." We'd like you to consider examining not just your head knowledge, but also your heart. Psalm 119:9-11 says:

> How can a young person stay on the path of purity? By living according to your word. I seek you with all my heart; do not let me stray from your commands. I have hidden your word in my heart that I might not sin against you.

We want you to commit to waiting for God's best *and* commit to seeking Him daily through reading and living His Word. Are you ready? You can use the prayer on the next page as an expression of your choice or as a prayer of commitment. Put a check mark by each of the ways you are committing to follow Christ and His path.

Path to Purity Prayer

Lord, I need Your guidance to stay on the path of purity. I want to follow Your Word and do what it says so I will be clean in Jesus Christ.

I commit to seek You and listen for Your voice every day. I will follow Your commands with my head and with my heart.

Guide me with Your presence and help me remember Your Word so I can call on Your wisdom day and night.

Thank You that Your Word is my protection and shield. Your promises are perfect, and I trust in You alone. Thank You for being my loving and perfect God. Help me make You my priority each day.

I commit to:

❏ Honor the Lord with my body.

❏ Learn God's Word and hide it in my heart.

❏ Seek God's truths by renewing my mind daily in His Word.

❏ Keep my eyes on the things of God instead of earthly things.

_____   _____
(your name)   (date)

Personal Reflections

1. Are the hopes you wrote down under "The Perfect Prom Date" realistic? Why or why not?

2. What is the difference between "Mr. Righteous" and "Mr. Right Now"?

3. How important to you is dating a guy who places God first in his life?

4. How can you tell when God is a priority in someone's life?

5. Was the story of Hosea and Gomer new to you? What did you learn about Hosea's faithfulness? What did you learn about God's faithfulness?

6. Have you experienced the trauma of parents who divorced? Or have you experienced another event that rocked your world? If yes, how can you see God in the midst of it? We encourage you to write in a journal every day, including at least one thing you are grateful for.

7. How has this chapter helped change or update your perspective on the qualities you want in a guy?

TEARS, FEARS, AND DRAMA—OH MY!

THE EMOTIONAL QUOTIENT

Emotional: *Being by nature easily affected by or quick to express emotions; inspired or governed by emotion rather than reason or willpower.*

Emotions. Girls and emotions. One minute you might be hysterically laughing, and the next you're hysterically crying. Why is that? While guys tend to have the ability to hide their feelings, most of the time we can tell how a girl feels just by looking at her face.

Think back over the past couple of days. Circle the emotions you experienced. Feel free to add emotions you've experienced if they're not listed.

sad silly happy angry thoughtful stressed

tired fearful guilty embarrassed

attracted frustrated hopeful enthusiastic envious

surprised disgusted ashamed lonely prideful

anxious grateful panicked love

How many words did you circle? Are you surprised at the number of emotions you can experience in just a few days? No wonder girls get labeled "the emotional gender"!

We know guys experience the same types of emotions. But the way they respond to their emotions is quite different than most girls. Girls prefer to express emotional eruptions with "interaction," while guys tend to handle emotions with "action." Have you ever noticed that?

Think back to the last time you were angry about a situation. For instance, maybe your younger sister took your favorite T-shirt and wore it to school. Later you discover she had taken the shirt and spilled Coke down the front. How did you react? Most girls would go straight to their moms and complain or tell all their friends about their horrible sister. They might even express their anger online so all their friends would know.

Now, let's change the situation up a bit. This time instead of the situation involving sisters, the same scenario happens with brothers. The T-shirt is still borrowed without permission and stained. Boys might still complain to their moms, but it will be with greater intensity. Instead of a whiny voice, boys might yell. An older brother might also retaliate with action. He might grab one of his brother's shirts and mess it up or he might shove his younger brother around.

We're not making a judgment call on either response. We just want to make sure you realize the difference in the ways guys and girls usually respond. Remember, girls "interact," which means they usually want to be heard. Guys want "action," which means they usually respond physically. This knowledge is crucial when it comes to dating. There will be times when guys won't want to "talk" about the drama of the day. They just want to act on it and move on.

Boys do have feelings. While they may portray themselves as tough, they do get emotional. When we asked some guys, "What's one thing you want girls to know about you?" one of the most common responses was, "Let girls know we have feelings too." Guys will experience the same kind of rejection and heartache you will. They will probably just show it differently.

Emotional Quotient Quiz

Are you a drama queen? Have you ever given a 50-cent event a 500-dollar reaction? How do you usually respond or react in stressful situations? Take a moment and complete the "Emotional Quotient Quiz." Circle the response you would normally have in each situation.

(You can also go to our Website www.withunveiledfaces.com and do the quiz online.)

Emotional Quotient Quiz

1. You just found out a really cute boy from your church likes your best friend. He asks you not to say anything.

   A. You go ahead and tell your friend everything. She would want to know.

   B. You promise not to say anything, but when you see your girlfriend you give her hints so she can figure it out.

   C. You tell the guy that she's not right for him because you want him to like you instead.

   D. You keep the secret, hoping for the best for both friends.

2. One of the girls on your softball team gets nominated to be captain. You know she parties on the weekends.

   A. You start a rumor that she got drunk over the weekend, hoping the coach will replace her.

   B. You complain to your friends and bad-mouth the girl in front of as many people as you can.

   C. You become friends with her so you'll get more attention from the coach.

   D. You pray for her—that she will be successful as captain and that God will give you opportunities to share Christ with her.

3. You know you can sing better than the girl who got chosen to lead worship in the student ministry band.

   A. Every time the girl leads worship, you make fun of her to your friends and refuse to sing.

   B. You decide to stop going to church on Wednesday nights. That'll teach the youth minister.

C. You compliment the girl to her face, but you don't really mean it. Inside you're envious.

D. You realize worship isn't about the person leading, but about honoring and praising God. You decide that's more important than leading the worship yourself.

4. There's an exchange student at school who doesn't speak English very well. It's been hard for her to make friends.

   A. Some of your friends at lunch talk about how strange she is and how odd her clothes are. You join in.

   B. You ignore her. Why should you have to be the one who includes the new girl?

   C. You are nice to the girl because you feel sorry for her.

   D. You invite her to sit with you at lunch. You ask her to come with you to church so she can learn about the Bible. You pray for opportunities to share Christ with her.

5. One of your friends is having sex with her boyfriend and finds out she's pregnant.

   A. Your attitude is "What was she thinking? She knew it was wrong, she knew the consequences, and now she's paying for her wrong decision."

   B. You distance yourself from her. If people think you're friends, they might assume you're having sex with your boyfriend too.

   C. You're nice to her on the outside, but inside you believe she's getting what she deserves for making such a dumb decision.

   D. You realize her situation must be really hard. You reach out to encourage her. You allow her to express what she's going through, keep what she says private, and stand by her side during the tough times.

Look over the quiz and count how many A's, B's, C's, and D's you circled:

_____ A's   _____ B's   _____ C's   _____ D's

If you circled mostly A's, then consider evaluating your emotions and how you respond. You tend toward letting drama get the best of you, which can ruin good relationships.

If you circled mostly B's, you might tend to secretly want revenge. Check your motives and ask God to guide your responses.

If you answered mostly C's, you tend to say one thing but think another. You look like you care on the outside, but you still have some issues to work through on the inside.

If you answered mostly D's, you're on your way to understanding how to respond in kindness and with a Christlike attitude. You might not always know how to respond the best way, but you seek to have the mind of Christ.

from Robin...

Homecoming Shocker

It was homecoming night during my junior year of high school. I was a cheerleader, and my boyfriend Ronnie was quarterback of the football team. He was leading the team down the field toward another touchdown. My friends and I were elated. We were winning, life seemed great, and we were anticipating the homecoming dance following the game. I had it all planned out. I would change into my new dress as soon as the game was over. Then I would waltz into the homecoming dance with Ronnie by my side.

Things quickly changed during the fourth quarter. Cheering on the sidelines, I had a good view of the crowd. That's when I saw her. In the midst of hundreds of screaming fans yelling for our Eagles, I spotted a cute sophomore who had on a familiar jacket. It was a letter jacket with Ronnie's #7 on the sleeves. He'd given her his letter jacket to wear to the homecoming game!

I was fuming from head to toe. How could he! How could she! It was the ultimate betrayal—me on the sidelines cheering and being the last to know Ronnie had homecoming plans that didn't include me. As you can guess, the dance didn't go so well. After four years of dating, my relationship with Ronnie ended in my driveway that night. I also wanted to make sure everyone knew how badly I'd been wronged.

Sadly, most everyone else already knew what was happening. The drama of the day left me heartbroken and embarrassed.

I've learned a lot since then about discerning when someone isn't telling the truth or a situation isn't quite right. Being in the broadcasting business for close to 30 years, I love gathering the details for news stories, and I've developed "street smarts" when it comes to getting the information I need for a story. Too bad I wasn't able to figure that out on the football sidelines. I could have saved myself a lot of misery. If only I'd learned how to not let someone rob me of joy back then.

A Tale of Two Women

If you think drama between girls and women is recent history, think again. There's been goings-on between us girls since the beginning. One of the earliest stories of girl drama is reported in the book of Genesis, and it involves three people: Abraham (Abram), Sarah (Sarai), and Hagar.

The story actually begins in Genesis 15 when God makes a covenant with Abraham. God promises Abraham that he will have descendants as numerous as the stars. There was one big problem—Abraham and his wife, Sarah, couldn't get pregnant. And they weren't getting any younger! He was 75 and Sarah was 65—older than many of your grandparents.

Sarah responds by taking matters into her own hands—something we girls tend to be really good at. When God doesn't come through for us during *our* timetable, we wonder if He might need a little help. It was a bad idea for Sarah, and it's still a bad idea today.

Because Sarah couldn't get pregnant, she made the decision to get her servant Hagar to step in as a substitute or surrogate mother (Genesis 16:1-3 NLT). She probably thought Hagar would carry the baby, and then she would "adopt" and raise him as her own. Can you imagine encouraging another woman to have sex with your husband so she could get pregnant? And Hagar was probably a teenager. It seems farfetched to most of us, but Sarah was desperate and lacked faith in God's promise. The consequences of her actions were severe.

Hagar gets pregnant, and the drama really unfolds. We learn that when Sarah finds out Hagar is pregnant, she becomes jealous. What seemed like a good idea at the beginning now seems like a terrible one.

To top it off, Hagar taunts Sarah about being barren. Sarah blames Abraham and mistreats Hagar. Oh the drama! Oh the tears!

Hagar runs away into the desert. She's despondent and alone. An "angel of the LORD" appears and reassures Hagar she will have a son who will have numerous descendants, although the descendants will live in hostility with others. He tells Hagar to return to Abraham's house, which she does. Then Ishmael is born.

The drama continues 14 years later, after Isaac is born to Abraham and Sarah. Isaac was the son God promised Abraham and Sarah. They were 100 and 90 years old, respectively, when their son was born. They named him Isaac, which means "laughter." Surely there was a lot of joy when Isaac arrived!

But Hagar and Ishmael aren't laughing. They became a constant irritation to Isaac and Sarah. The mama bear in Sarah finally roars. She gives Hagar and Ishmael their walking papers and tells them to never come back. Sarah's actions still affect our world today. How? The birth of the Islamic religion probably stems from the bloodline of Ishmael, while Christianity comes about through the descendants of Isaac. As you know, there is still much conflict in the world between Islam and Christianity.

What can we learn from the story about Abraham, Sarah, and Hagar? We can trust God and His plans. We need to make sure we don't take matters into our own hands. We can avoid acting like Hagar and Sarah when we disagree. And we can strive to respond more lovingly with our word choices, which is a biggie for most of us verbal females.

Watching Our Words

The Bible has a lot to say about the way we use our words and the power of our tongues. Let's look at the biggest area that tends to get us girls in trouble—gossip. The definition of "gossip" is most often described as "a conversation that involves rumors or facts with the intent to be hurtful or harm someone." Whether your conversation is true or not, if you're spreading personal information about someone else, you're probably guilty of gossip. Here are a few verses from Scripture that will help us define gossip even further.

- *Proverbs 11:13:* "A gossip betrays a confidence, but a trustworthy person keeps a secret." When we share secrets with someone, we're gossiping!

- *Proverbs 16:28:* "A perverse person stirs up conflict, and a gossip separates close friends." When we talk about others in a way that causes conflict between friends, it's gossip. When words cause division, especially between believers, it's probably gossip.

- *Proverbs 26:20:* "Without wood a fire goes out; without a gossip a quarrel dies down." Have you had two friends who were arguing? Instead of keeping it between them, you decide to take sides and provide ammunition, so you speak up. That's called "adding fuel to the fire," and it's destructive. If you're contributing to gossip, that makes you a gossip.

- *1 Timothy 5:13:* "Not only do they become idlers, but also busybodies who talk nonsense, saying things they ought not to." When was the last time you brought up a subject that wasn't honoring to the Lord? For instance, maybe your conversation focused on something someone was doing that you didn't like or you thought wasn't good. If you enjoy spending time talking about others, you are a gossip.

How to Stop the Gossip

Let's face it, you're going to be around people who gossip for the rest of your life. And most of us (okay, probably all of us), are guilty of gossip at times. How you handle this topic will affect the way you relate to others, especially the guys you are interested in.

First, when you hear gossip or a rumor, walk away. Seriously! Just walk away. The more you hear, the more you are going to be tempted to share the information with someone else.

Second, confront the gossiper in truth and love. If you're with a friend who is sharing a secret, say, "I'm really uncomfortable with this conversation. Can we change the subject?" If possible, do this quietly or privately. You don't have to throw a Bible in her face, but if needed, gently remind her that she wouldn't want someone to share secrets about her.

Finally, let the gossip end with you. This can be the hardest part. You've heard news, so you want to share it with someone. Instead, will you learn to keep your mouth shut and keep the information to yourself?

Yes, we understand the power of spreading news. Both of us are in the news business, and we see the impact of living in a world of instant communication and instant news all the time.

When Apple founder Steve Jobs passed away, word spread quickly, mostly through the devices he helped create—the iPhone and iPad. With social networking tools, including Facebook and Twitter, the announcement of Jobs' passing was faster than "breaking news" could be aired on the official, more traditional media stations. It was instant information.

We see the power of being in the "know" each day because we work in an environment where urgency is the atmosphere. It's a contagious adrenaline rush to see how fast we can get information to the public. Whether it's sending a reporter out to the scene live or sending the weather team out to find the nearest tornado, information gathered can be powerful.

The problem is that sometimes in the rush to deliver the news, it's easy to get misinformation. We work hard to make sure our sources are reliable and credible. We know that rumors are not facts, and our credibility as journalists will be harmed if we report inaccurate information.

We should be able to say the same for everyone's conversations. Colossians 4:6 says, "Let your conversation be always full of grace, seasoned with salt, so that you may know how to answer everyone."

Control the Fire

Does it seem that girls are more wrapped up in drama than guys? Whether it's a desire to be in the know or a craving to be part of the conversation, drama can lead to heartache and heartbreak, especially when it involves relationships.

The Bible is pretty clear about the damage our tongues can do. James 3:5-6 says:

> The tongue is a small part of the body, but it makes great boasts. Consider what a great forest is set on fire by a small spark. The tongue also is a fire, a world of evil among the parts of the body. It corrupts the whole body, sets the

whole course of one's life on fire, and is itself set on fire
by hell.

Have you thought about the comparison between a fire and our
tongues? Fires cause major damage, and so can our tongues when we
speak in ways that don't honor God. Because our words can get us
into trouble, we must learn self-control. When we hear gossip, change
the subject. Instead of tearing someone down, choose words that build
someone up. If we can overcome our urge to gossip, we can avoid some
of the dramas that can damage our guy relationships.

Psalm 35:28 says, "My tongue will proclaim your righteousness [LORD], your praises all day long." Next time your girlfriends get
together for a gabfest of juicy gossip, remember that you have a choice
in the way you respond. Choose to use your tongue as a megaphone to
shout God's goodness. Forest fires are easy to prevent but hard to put
out once the blaze begins.

Let's say good-bye to drama and hello to self-control.

Personal Reflections

1. Did you take the Emotional Quotient Quiz? Were you surprised at how many emotions you experienced in a short time? What did you learn about yourself?

2. Are you a drama queen? Why or why not? How can you avoid some of the drama between friends?

3. Consider Sarah and Hagar's situation. Describe a time in a friendship when you tried to take control of a situation instead of waiting for God's plan to unfold. What happened?

4. What did you learn from Sarah and Hagar that will help you avoid some dramas?

5. Have you ever been the subject of gossip? If yes, how did you feel about it?

6. What will you do the next time you're around someone who is gossiping?

7. Why is it easier to start gossip than to stop it?

HOW FAR IS TOO FAR?

SETTING BOUNDARIES

Boundary: *The point at which something ends or beyond which it becomes something else.*

Whether you realize it or not, there have been boundaries in your life since the time you were born. Before you came home from the hospital, your parents considered your surroundings and made sure the house was safe and secure for you. The crib you slept in probably had bumper pads to protect you and high sides to keep you from falling out.

As you got older, the boundaries broadened to cover the new activities and challenges you faced. When you went outside, you were told where you could go and where you couldn't. You knew where you could ride your bike and what kind of helmet was required.

When teens get driver's licenses, they are given more freedom and privileges, but also new boundaries. Your parents provide restrictions, and so does the government. There are boundaries for when you can drive, how fast you can go, and which direction to drive. You follow instructions on signs and stop when the lights are red. If you don't, disaster is imminent.

Boundaries are not bad. They provide protection and give you guidelines to avoid potential harm. Just like an umbrella provides protection from the rain, God's boundaries provide protection for your present and future relationships.

We're entering a chapter that is sure to capture your attention. Why? Because it addresses a question girls always ask and think about when it comes to dating and physical attraction: How far is too far? Where do I set the line? Does the line change? What is God's boundary regarding physical contact in dating and love?

Let's get something out of the way first. If you're looking for us to give you permission to go to a certain point or specific guidelines regarding where you stop with a boy when it comes to physical contact, you're not going to find it. Don't be disappointed. We are going to look at some steps of physical progression in dating. And we're going to share some principles from Scripture that will give you God's wisdom in this area instead of just offering our opinion. We believe God has given all of us a standard of purity. And He has given all of us the ability to use self-control. Our hope is that you won't let the world dictate to you what the sexual norms are for teenagers. Our prayer is that you'll allow the Holy Spirit to teach and lead you, providing God's hedge of protection around your life.

from Lauren...
The Line Before the Line

When I met Randy, I knew things were going to be different. Just prior to our meeting, I'd ended a pretty rough relationship. I decided I was done with guys for a while, and I had no plans to date anyone seriously for a long time. I was ready to celebrate being single and hang out with my friends...or so I thought.

Several people told me I would find "the one" when I least expected it. I didn't believe them until I started dating Randy.

I know this might seem crazy, but on our first date I knew this was the man I wanted to spend the rest of my life with. Knowing how much I was attracted to him, I was concerned that it might be very difficult to keep appropriate physical boundaries in place.

Thankfully, Randy was forthright and honest with me about how to set godly physical boundaries. We talked openly about the lines we didn't want to cross, and we promised each other to be strong in sticking to them.

One tool that helped us keep our commitments was attending a college Bible study on setting and honoring physical boundaries. We learned how to set a "line *before* the line." In other words, we set a physical boundary line that was a step before what we thought it should be. For example, if our physical boundary was kissing on the mouth, then we would stop with a kiss on the cheek. The idea of stopping at the "line before the line" gave us extra protection against going further than we wanted to go when passion tried to overwhelm logic.

I'm so grateful for the stand Randy took in our relationship. I'm even more grateful that he had kept the same sexual purity standards in his past relationships. It showed that he cared more about me than instant gratification. He respected the girls he dated, and he wanted to honor God and stay pure for his future wife. I also learned the importance of not just letting things "happen," but actively talking to each other and setting boundaries before our relationship progressed very far. We also agreed on the boundaries and supported each other.

Setting boundaries is all about planning and being prepared. If you wait until you're in the heat of the moment to set a standard, the chances are the situation will go further than you planned to go. Let "Be Prepared and Ready" be your motto.

Please hear me out. No guy should ever ask you to do something physically that doesn't match up with God's best for you. Ephesians 5:28 says, "Husbands ought to love their wives as their own bodies. He who loves his wife loves himself." Relationships are a two-way street. Remember, while his responsibility is to help you stay pure and holy, you are accountable to help your brother in Christ not stumble by what you wear, what you say, and what you do.

Because of our discipline in this area, I know my marriage to Randy is stronger. And we have no regrets or guilt because we didn't cross God's standard for purity.

Let's Get Physical

God created you—body, soul, and spirit. Because He created you with a physical body and a desire for relationships, it is natural to want physical contact with a guy. It's perfectly normal for you to think about holding hands, kissing, and being intimate with the opposite sex. We believe sex is a wonderful gift from the Lord. That said, also know that God has set a boundary for sex: within a marriage relationship only.

The way you treat your physical body is often a reflection of the spiritual condition of your heart. Several years ago, Dr. James Dobson published a book on the progression of physical intimacy called *Love for a Lifetime*. The first eight steps are generally seen as natural physical progressions during dating, while steps 9 through 12 are reserved for marriage. Here are his steps, along with our insights.

Step 1: Eye to body. What attracts you first to a guy? We know that personality and their walk with the Lord are priorities, but the simple truth is that you are usually first attracted to a guy by the way he looks. And sometimes his outward appearance can give you a glimpse of his inward personality or even his closeness with God. The same is true for how guys become attracted to you. They tend to be more visual than girls, which means they are generally first attracted by physical appearance. Think about the guys you think are cute. What was the first thing you noticed about them? Was it their curly hair? Maybe their smile? Sounds kind of superficial, doesn't it? But the truth is that a "first look" might turn into a second or a third.

Step 2: Eye to eye. Have you ever looked at a guy, and when he looked back, you turned bright red? When your eyes meet, your face feels warm and a smile appears. Those are nonverbal signals that say, "I might want to know you better." You might even think, "He actually noticed me!"

Step 3: Voice to voice. After you notice someone, the next natural step is engaging in conversation. It might be as simple as "What's your name?" or "What subjects do you like in school?" This should be one of the longest stages in getting to know someone. Remember earlier when we mentioned "talking" or "texting"? While that is one form of conversation, it isn't the same as actually talking voice to voice.

This step is considered a friendship phase, and it's one of the most important stages of physical attraction. Even when you start going out with a guy one-on-one, you will (hopefully) spend a lot more time talking than anything you do physically. And someday when you're married, the same will also hold true. So enjoy conversations with the guy you are dating.

Step 4: Hand to hand. Have you ever sat next to a guy that you liked and wished he would hold your hand? If you're like most girls we know, you casually made sure your hand was by your side—just waiting for the right moment. (FYI: A lot of guys don't get the hint!) If you've held hands with a guy you're interested in, you know that special feeling you get when your relationship has definitely taken the next step. The more you hold hands, the greater the romantic attachment becomes.

Step 5: Hand to shoulder. Think of this classic scene. Boy and girl are sitting next to each other in a movie. The boy wants to put his arm around the girl, and the girl is secretly hoping he will. Then comes the infamous fake stretch and yawn by the boy, and his arm comes down and settles around the girl's shoulder. You are together but facing forward.

This step reveals that your relationship is more than a casual friendship. There's also something else to be aware of at this point. Some girls refer to this as a "cuddling" stage. It can open the door to the next step of physical intimacy. When you let a guy put his arm on your shoulder or around your shoulder, you're communicating that you like him and want a deeper connection, including the eventual possibility of physical intimacy.

Step 6: Hand to waist. When you're walking arm-in-arm or with your hands around each other's waist, you're in a position to share private conversations. You are side-by-side but still mostly facing forward.

Step 7: Face to face. This level of physical attraction is a big step in dating. You're gazing into each other's eyes, hugging and kissing. We believe this step should be taken only after a significant amount of time has passed. By this point, you've had a boundary-setting conversation with your parents and then with the guy.

Many girls have convictions about setting the boundary to not kiss. But we also know many of you will probably reach this stage, and this is a personal decision you need to pray about. Because kissing involves communication without words, there are lots of physical impulses that can quickly get out of control. If you decide to kiss, be aware that it heightens sexual attraction for both of you and stimulates physical responses. It doesn't take much for a boy to be physically aroused, and face-to-face intimacy will definitely cause a guy to have to deal with sexual feelings. For girls, face-to-face contact arouses physical sensations, but also emotional feelings. Girls become emotionally attached much sooner than guys, which can be a turn-off to them. When girls kiss, their thoughts can easily turn to relationship, playing house, and putting up picket fences. When boys kiss, their thoughts turn toward sex.

Step 8: Hand to head. Rarely do people touch each other's heads unless they are romantically involved or if they are someone in your family. This is a sign of affection that signifies a close connection or intimacy.

Steps 9 through 12. The final steps of physical involvement. These are reserved for marriage. They are more sexual and private. Most believers agree these steps are boundaries not to cross in a dating relationship. They include *Step 9: Hand to body, Step 10: Mouth to breast, Step 11: Touching below the waist,* and *Step 12: Sexual intercourse.*[6]

Run—Don't Walk

One of the most amazing stories of setting physical boundaries is found in Genesis. The central character is Joseph, the son of Jacob and Rachel. You might know the story of Joseph. His father gave him a beautiful, special coat that revealed Joseph was the favored son. And Joseph dreamed his brothers would eventually bow down to him. Needless to say, Joseph's brothers were very jealous. They finally set out for revenge. In a moment of anger, his brothers sold him as a slave to people in a passing caravan.

Obviously Joseph's life changed drastically. But in the midst of captivity, God was working in Joseph's life. After being a slave for a long time, Joseph's integrity garnered him an appointment as a trusted advisor in a nobleman's house. There his character was tested greatly.

Joseph found himself living in the house of Potiphar, an officer of the Pharaoh of Egypt. Although Joseph was still a slave, we get a glimpse of God's protection and love for him:

> The LORD was with Joseph so that he prospered, and he
> lived in the house of his Egyptian master. When his master
> saw that the LORD was with him and that the LORD gave
> him success in everything he did, Joseph found favor in his
> eyes and became his attendant. Potiphar put him in charge
> of his household, and he entrusted to his care everything
> he owned (Genesis 39:2-4).

Potiphar's house was blessed because of Joseph's faithfulness to the Lord. Have you ever considered that your faithfulness to the Lord could be a blessing to someone who is an authority figure in your life? This might be your parents, a teacher, a youth minister, or someone you work for.

But back to Joseph, who really needs to hang on to his toga! Potiphar's wife has taken notice of him. Scripture says Joseph was well-built and handsome. Very few men in the Bible are described this way. Potiphar's wife was definitely attracted to Joseph physically.

Consider for a moment how Joseph's character and his relationship with the Lord also made him appealing. A man's relationship with God gives him a confidence that can be seen. A man whose spiritual walk is on track is thoughtful, kind, and generous. And since God designed us to be responders to men, this makes a man even more appealing. We don't know why Potiphar's wife was looking for love outside her marriage, but since Potiphar was Egyptian, it's a good guess that neither of them was following the one true God.

Whether she was lonely or just aggressive, Potiphar's wife was a cougar on the prowl. She took notice of Joseph and set out to have a sexual relationship with him. And there were no subtle hints here. She didn't keep her feelings or intentions hidden. "Now Joseph was well-built and handsome, and after a while his master's wife took notice of Joseph and said, 'Come to bed with me!'" (Genesis 39:6-7).

Joseph refused, but she persisted. The Bible said she went after him day after day. Finally, Potiphar's wife schemed an opportune time when the other servants were away. She physically grabbed Joseph. In one quick move, Joseph fled the scene, but the woman had yanked his cloak off and held on to it (verse 12).

There are several important insights we can learn from Joseph and how he handled the situation.

Joseph was careful to not be alone in a tempting situation. Because Potiphar's wife specifically had to make sure no one was around in the final scene, it's safe to say that when she made advances to him in previous times, other servants were in the house. And since we know Joseph was an honorable man, it's reasonable to assume he also made sure he was never alone with his master's wife, especially once he knew her intentions.

What does this have to do with you? If you want to place a safeguard on your physical boundaries, avoid situations where you are alone with a guy. Never invite a guy over or to come into your house without a parent present. Make a conscious decision to not park in secluded areas or popular make-out locations. When you're watching a movie together at his house or yours, don't cover yourselves with a blanket where inappropriate touching can occur unseen.

Keeping within a group of people engaged in nonsexual activities is one of the easiest ways to maintain physical boundaries. Remember Ephesians 5:3: "Among you there must not be even a hint of sexual immorality, or of any kind of impurity, or of greed, because these are improper for God's holy people." When you're alone with a guy, it's too easy to push the boundaries or cross a line by getting caught up in emotions and sensations.

Joseph called the temptation what it was—sin. Joseph said to Potiphar's wife, "How then could I do such a wicked thing and sin against God?" Instead of the pot calling the kettle black, Joseph called Pot's wife out! Sometimes, girls, it's easy to justify sin and cover it up as harmless. You might try to justify crossing a physical boundary, but don't be fooled. Maybe you are thinking, "Well, we haven't had sex, so our messing around really doesn't count. Right?" Wrong. Sin is sin. Joseph knew that if he crossed this line, his sin would affect his master, himself, his situation, and, most important, his relationship with God.

When faced with a blatant advance, Joseph ran. Did you notice that? Joseph didn't casually make excuses and continue talking when Potiphar's wife came on to him. He left! He ran! He fled the scene as fast as he could. God promises you that He will *always* provide a way of escape when you face any temptation: "No temptation has overtaken you except what is common to mankind. And God is faithful; he will not let you be tempted beyond what you can bear. But when you are tempted, he will also provide a way out so that you can endure it" (1 Corinthians 10:13).

Although God provides a way out, you have to be willing to take it! So do you know what to look for? The way out may come in avenues you don't expect. It may be your mom coming to check on you. It may be the phone ringing while you are in the heat of the moment. It may be the Holy Spirit warning your head and heart, "You are in dangerous territory!" No matter how it comes, recognize that God is giving you a way out of the tempting situation. If you are faced with a situation where you feel pressured by a guy to get physical, get out. Leave the situation as fast as you can.

Crossing the Line in Your Mind

It's simple to distinguish physical boundaries when it comes to sexual sin. But Jesus took it further when He addressed the sin that occurs without even holding hands: "You have heard that it was said, 'You shall not commit adultery.' But I tell you that anyone who looks at a woman lustfully has already committed adultery with her in his heart" (Matthew 5:27-28). Jesus wasn't speaking of physically crossing a boundary, He was speaking of crossing a boundary in your mind. Another word that describes what Jesus is talking about is "lust." Lust can be described as "intense sexual desire, or a passionate or overmastering desire or craving." "Overmastering" means lust becomes the "master" of your desire instead of God.

Lust is a secret sin hidden in the recesses of the mind. It may stem from seeing pictures on the Internet that lure you in. It might spark when a cute guy in math class flirts with you using sweet words. Your mind can run wild after a casual touch from a guy's hand. The landmines come in ways that can touch all five of your senses. That's the dangerous thing about lust. It overtakes your thoughts and affects your actions. So how can you stand against it? How can you not sin in this area?

God's Word is your lifeline. One of the most important spiritual disciplines you can develop is memorizing Scripture. When you hide God's Word in your heart, you'll be able to withstand the pressures of lust—and a lot of other temptations—because God's wisdom and strength will come to you to use as a shield. Are you wondering where to start? Here are some great verses to memorize.

- *2 Corinthians 10:5:* "We demolish arguments and every pretension [claim] that sets itself up against the knowledge of God, and we take captive every thought to make it obedient to Christ."

- *Ephesians 5:15-16:* "Be very careful, then, how you live—not as unwise but as wise, making the most of every opportunity, because the days are evil."

- *Philippians 4:8:* "Whatever is true, whatever is noble, whatever is right, whatever is pure, whatever is lovely, whatever is admirable—if anything is excellent or praiseworthy—think about such things."

Practical Reasons

We've given you a lot of spiritual reasons why you should carefully guard yourself to maintain godly physical boundaries when it comes to interactions with guys. But there are also practical reasons why sex before marriage is not a good idea.

Pregnancy. Approximately 1,100 teenage girls give birth *each day* in the United States. That means 1 out of every 10 new mothers is a teenager.[2] Here's an interesting and important fact: No birth control method outside of abstinence is foolproof.

Sexually transmitted diseases (STDs). Of the 12 million cases of STDs diagnosed each year, 3 million are among teenagers. Approximately 13 percent of youth ages 13 to 19 contract an STD each year.[3] Your health can be seriously affected by an STD. It can lead to infertility, pregnancy complications in the future, blindness, certain types of cancers, and even death.

Depression and suicide. Studies have shown that sexually active teens are more likely to experience depression or attempt suicide.[4] It's hard for teens to prepare for and deal with the emotional attachment of being intimate with someone, especially if the relationship ends. Many teens experience negative emotional consequences, such as feeling used or bad about themselves. Low self-esteem can lead to more risky behavior, which can lead to guilt and depression.

Difficult to backtrack. We're not saying if you've gone too far physically with a guy that you can't take a step back, reset your physical standards, and continue with a more godly relationship. You can, but it's not easy. Once you've allowed yourself to experience something intimate with someone, both of you will struggle with the strong desire to cross the line again.

from Robin...
Keep Her Holy

My first impression of Keith was "Wow! What a manly man!" He definitely caught my eye. A woman friend who had extremely good taste set us up on a blind date. I was not disappointed. Keith, on the outside, had everything I wanted and thought I needed. He was good-looking, strong in physical appearance, and I liked the way he walked with confidence. But something he did on our first date allowed me to get a glimpse into his even stronger heart for God.

He handed me a gift and told me it was something that would help me know a little bit more about who he was as a man. My curiosity was piqued. When I opened the package, I discovered the book *Wild at Heart* by John Eldredge. Eldredge does a masterful job of describing God's design for men—warriors, heroes, and spiritual beings filled with the desire to be providers. How appealing this sounded to me.

I hadn't known if I would ever be able to find love again, especially after having my heart broken. I was a 40-year-old single mom who had a lot of questions for God about dating again. I had enjoyed all the physical freedoms of marriage, and now I was back to setting physical boundaries. Truthfully, I was nervous. I wrote in my journal, "Lord, help me stay pure in my thoughts and actions."

Keith and I started spending more time together, and we developed strong feelings for each other. We prayed and asked the Lord if we were following Him in our relationship. Our first kiss was two months into our dating relationship. We set boundary lines, and as our relationship grew deeper, we talked about how we were going to handle physical temptation.

Keith called me one day and shared with me that God woke him in the middle of the night and said, "Robin is precious to me. Keep her holy." Keith told me he wanted to honor the Lord in this area of our relationship. I knew he was the man for me because he did! Keith kept a handle on his desires and treated me with care and respect. We dated for exactly a year, and we've been happily married for several years.

Have You Crossed the Line?

Maybe you've messed up in the way you handled the physical part of dating. First, you're not alone. This is a difficult area for everyone, male and female. And we have messed up too. We encourage you to set the boundaries again and move forward from this point on. And keep reading! We serve a God who offers forgiveness and hope, and we're going to help you look to Him for strength and courage.

Personal Reflections

1. Do you like to push the boundaries? If yes, what areas do you struggle with and need to be on guard for?

2. How do boundaries protect you physically, emotionally, and spiritually?

3. Have you established physical boundaries for dating? If yes, what are they? If no, what steps will you put in place now to keep you safe? Who can you go to for help in establishing godly boundaries?

4. If you were in a similar situation to Joseph's, what would you do? How do you think God would provide a way out? How would you recognize it?

5. What is your part when it comes to escaping temptation?

I'VE MESSED UP, NOW WHAT?

PAST REGRETS, FUTURE HOPE

- -

Forgive: *To excuse somebody for a mistake, misunderstanding, wrongdoing, or an inappropriateness.*

- -

S o you've messed up when it comes to physical boundaries in a dating relationship. Now what? The good news is you can begin right now with a clean slate because of God's mercy. Trust us. We know the guilt and shame that comes from mistakes and sin. But we also know God doesn't want you to stay there. We're going to look at three of God's greatest gifts for you: forgiveness, grace, and hope.

from Lauren...
When God Forgives

Have you ever thought, "If I could only make this team, I will be satisfied." Or maybe you've said, "If I could only date that guy, I would be happy." We live in a world that focuses on getting what we want and having the very best. We are bombarded with the lie that to be complete we need the right car, the right boyfriend, and to be part of the right group. But those are lies. And to top it off, without God nothing will provide lasting peace, happiness, and success.

During my time as Miss America, I found myself relying on a relationship to fill a void in my life. I'd started dating a guy a few months after I won the Miss Oklahoma contest, and we dated throughout my year as Miss America. As I traveled the country, I became so lonely. Even though I was surrounded by lots of people, I didn't have someone I could talk to heart to heart. I relied on that guy and our relationship to be my everything. I felt like he was the one consistent piece in my life besides my family, so I counted on him and that relationship to provide stability and peace.

Because I relied on him to fill the emptiness I was feeling, I found myself doing things I thought I would never do. I got into the drinking scene and went too far physically and emotionally with him. I made those mistakes because I was relying on him and our relationship to satisfy me instead of relying on God to fill my heart. The shame and guilt from some of the decisions I made in that relationship almost crippled me. I felt unworthy even to the point of believing I could never have a healthy relationship with another person or an intimate relationship with God.

Several months after that relationship ended, I reconnected with God. I began to grow spiritually again. Then I met Randy, and I knew immediately that I liked him. But like most girls, I worried if the guy I liked would return my feelings. One day, I spent all my waking moments wondering, "What if he doesn't like me?" and "What if he just wants to be friends?" After spending the whole day in a tizzy, I came home to an empty apartment with nothing to do. I got into my pajamas, flopped down on my bed, and started my Bible study. I found myself praying and breaking down before the Lord. I remember saying out loud, "God, You be my boyfriend until the right guy comes along. And if it isn't Randy, don't let him call me again." As soon as I said "Amen," the phone rang. It was Randy asking if I wanted to watch a movie. With tears still in my eyes from my breakdown with God, I quickly said "Yes!" Within ten minutes, I got out of my pajamas, wiped the tears from my face, and slapped on some makeup.

You've already heard me say that Randy is incredible, and I love being married to him. But even in the midst of being happily married, I realized soon after we were together that I was still holding on to the shame and guilt from the not-so-good decisions I'd made in the past. I continued to carry around a cloud of despair, so I wasn't walking in the full light of Christ.

When I fully gave my heart to Christ and asked Him to forgive me, I realized I needed to ask forgiveness from Randy too. Part of the reason I was still holding on to my disappointment about my past was because those decisions had ramifications for my marriage. Through tears, I asked Randy for forgiveness. His response overwhelmed me. He said he had already forgiven me, and that he would love me forever, no matter what.

It's amazing to me to see how God uses people to show us His unfailing love. The response I got from my husband is the same response we get from God when we repent. The shame and guilt I carried were lies that Satan, our enemy, wanted me to believe. I bought into the shame that God wouldn't give me a healthy relationship with a guy because of my past mistakes. I learned about God's faithfulness, forgiveness, and grace. I discovered He is ready to pick us up, dust us off, and hold us in His mighty and loving arms.

I share all of this to show you that even after the mistakes I made, after the times I turned from God and went down my own path, after the times that I said and did things that were in direct contradiction to what God asked of me, He was still with me. When I asked Him to step in and be my boyfriend, He did. And not only did He step in to be my boyfriend until the right guy came along, He gave me a husband that is beyond my wildest dreams.

In addition to learning about God's faithfulness to forgive, I learned about His faithfulness to forget. Psalm 103:11-12 says, "For as high as the heavens are above the earth, so great is his love for those who fear him; as far as the east is from the west, so far has he removed our transgressions from us." When we repent and turn from our sins, God casts them from His memory forever.

The Red Rope of Hope

The Bible is full of illustrations of God's forgiveness. In fact, that's really God's business—forgiveness and restoration. It's a continuing thread from the first words of Genesis all the way to the final words in Revelation. It's why God sent His Son! Through Jesus, God offered the world forgiveness and hope.

Although we could have chosen a lot of stories about forgiveness to share with you, we were particularly drawn to the story of the prostitute named Rahab. Her life reveals how God can take someone's mistakes and turn them into His masterpiece.

You'll find the beginning of Rahab's story in Joshua 2, when the Israelites are preparing to enter the Promised Land after leaving Egypt.

They had wandered 40 years in the desert, and with Joshua as their commander, God was giving them the green light to take the land. But first they would have to make a small stop in the "red light district," the place where prostitutes offered their bodies for money.

There are a lot of things we'd like to know about Rahab, but Scripture defines her only by her occupation—a harlot. No matter where you find her name in Scripture, that label follows.

Joshua sent two spies on a secret mission to inspect Jericho. "So they went and entered the house of a prostitute named Rahab and stayed there" (Joshua 2:1). Does it seem a little strange they would choose to stay in the home of a prostitute? Archaeologists reveal that her inn was most likely nestled *between* the double walls of Jericho. Men were probably seen entering and leaving on a regular basis. Two strange men knocking on her door would not have been suspicious.

The king of Jericho found out spies were around, and he instigated a search. He soon sent a message to Rahab: "Bring out the men who came to you and entered your house, because they have come to spy out the whole land" (Joshua 2:3). When the king's command reached Rahab, she was faced with a difficult choice—to expose the spies or to lie to the authorities. Bravely, Rahab makes a quick decision to protect the foreigners. She gives the classic reply, "I don't know which way they went. Go after them quickly" (verse 5).

Why did she lie? Isn't that a sin? Isn't it against one of the Ten Commandments? Apparently Rahab sensed that something spiritual was going on. She'd heard about the Israelites and the Egyptians and the Red Sea event. Maybe she was feeling empty by her pursuit of following pagan gods and idol worship. Whatever her reason, after hiding the men under stalks of flax on the rooftop, and after the searching soldiers leave, Rahab opens her heart to God. She tells the spies, "I know that the LORD has given you this land and that a great fear of you has fallen on us" (verse 9). Our courageous heroine proclaims her allegiance, "For the LORD your God is God in heaven above and on the earth below" (verse 11).

Wow! Rahab the prostitute is confessing that Jehovah God is the one true God! In her book *Bad Girls of the Bible,* Liz Curtis Higgs explains: "[Rahab had] seen the power of Jehovah God at work, accepted the reality of his existence, and confessed with her mouth to these witnesses that the One they called God was God, the almighty God."[1] Rahab's life was changed on earth and in heaven. She found forgiveness, grace, and hope for her future.

Because of her faith, the spies pledged to spare her family from the destruction that was coming. As she helped them escape, the spies gave her instructions to hang a red cord outside her window as a sign of protection. Red—a red rope in the red-light district. But for the Israelites, red symbolized the blood shed for forgiveness. It was the blood of the innocent lamb spread across the doorpost in Exodus to protect the Israelite children from death when Moses dealt with Pharaoh. It would eventually be the blood of the innocent man, Jesus, who would die for the sins of all people. For Rahab, red would no longer symbolize sin but the forgiveness and protection that would cover it.

As God promised, Jericho's walls fell. Rahab and her family were spared per the agreement the spies made. More important, Rahab was given new life. God forgave her past mistakes and wove her into the tapestry of His plan. When she left her house, she left everything behind, including her past.

And there's something really interesting about this story! Salmon, possibly one of the spies, saw beyond her past and loved Rahab. They married, and in the genealogy of Christ, we find this treasure: "Salmon the father of Boaz, whose mother was Rahab, Boaz the father of Obed, whose mother was Ruth, Obed the father of Jesse, and Jesse the father of King David" (Matthew 1:5-6). Not only was Rahab the mother of Boaz, who would later marry Ruth, but Rahab's name appears in the genealogy of Christ!

Her name also appears two other times in the New Testament—Hebrews 11:31 and James 2:24-25. In both passages, Rahab is still referred to as a prostitute. Why would the writers of the New Testament still call her that? Can't she get away from the label? Liz Curtis Higgs offers some insight: "Paul and James mentioned Rahab's past for the same reason people share their testimonies today—to demonstrate the 'before and after' power of knowing the Lord. Stories of how God has changed lives aren't intended to glorify sin; they are meant to glorify God's grace."[2]

How would Higgs know this? Because she, like Rahab, was a former "bad girl." And like Rahab, God got hold of her life. While she doesn't glorify her past, Liz Higgs tells her story to thousands of women each year in the hopes that her audiences will discover the same grace offered to her through Jesus Christ.

Remember, your past does not have to define your future. There is hope when you repent and turn to God. He will forgive!

from Robin...
A Child of the Heart

The story you're about to read is not my own. It's from a dear young woman I have the privilege of knowing. I'm so grateful she is willing to share her story with you. My prayer is that you'll read it and find compassion for other girls who find themselves in the same situation. If you're in the same situation my friend was in or you've been there before, I hope you'll understand how God offers His forgiveness and can use your testimony for His glory.

Ann's Story

I never thought it would happen to me. When you're a teen, you always hear stories of other girls getting pregnant. My perception was that those girls weren't very smart. I mean, how hard is it to refrain from sex until you're married? And if you're going to have sex, haven't you heard of condoms and birth control? But then it happened. I found out I was pregnant.

When I look back, I sometimes wonder how I got to that point. I was a bright, young girl with a promising future. And now I was one of "those" girls. One day I was a popular cheerleader, and the next day I was in a Burger King bathroom holding a pregnancy test. In a moment I realized my future was written on a thin piece of plastic with two bright blue lines. Positive.

Sex was not something my parents and I talked about much. Growing up in the home of a minister, I spent most of my life at church. I was only six years old when I asked Jesus to come into my heart. I'm not sure if I truly understood what it meant at the time, but I knew my parents would be pleased if I did it. I made the long trip down the aisle of the church and was baptized a week later.

And it wasn't that my mom didn't try to talk to me about sex. When I was 11, my mom asked me if I knew what sex was. Multiple friends had already informed me, so I nodded and prayed that was the end of the conversation. Nope. My mom continued to give me the details about the physical mechanics of sex. *Awkward.* Not knowing how to respond, I just laughed. Mom laughed as well. She explained that sex was wonderful (awkward again), but it was meant to be between a husband and wife only.

We didn't speak of it again until I was 13. My youth group went through "True Love Waits," a youth-based international campaign for refraining from premarital sex, and the final night was a dinner party for parents and their teens.[3] My dad gave me a purity ring and told me to wear it on my left ring finger. It would symbolize my commitment to abstain from sex until my wedding night. From that moment on, I was the poster child for purity. I didn't hide the fact that I was going to wait until marriage. I was proud of it.

And then I met Darren. He was a senior when I was a sophomore. He was popular and president of our large high school's student council. I was 15 when a friend introduced us. We immediately hit it off. We did all the right things. We were friends first. We hung out at my house with my parents. We played video games, and I taught him how to play the guitar. Everything was very innocent.

I never planned on having sex with Darren. We even talked about not doing it. On our first date, he asked me if I was a virgin. I told him I was, and that I was planning on staying that way until I married. Because he was older, I worried that he might think I was uptight or a prude. Much to my relief, he said he respected my decision, and he would never ask me to do anything I didn't want to do.

I can't remember when or where it happened. I only remember that we were often alone when we shouldn't have been. Each time we were together, we went a little further until one night we finally did it. I remember thinking that since I was no longer a virgin, there was nothing left for me to save so it was okay to keep on doing it as long as it was with him and no one else.

He graduated from high school and went to college in another state. Because we didn't want the pressure of a long-distance relationship, we broke up. Soon after he left for college, I was in the bathroom stall at Burger King. Waiting for the results of the pregnancy test seemed like an eternity. When the test was positive, I thought it couldn't be right. I bought two more tests. All of them came out positive.

That time was like a bad dream. I wanted to wake up, gasp for air, cling to my pillow, and be thankful life was back to normal. Only it wasn't a dream. It was very real. I couldn't sleep. I couldn't eat. What was going to happen to me? How was I going to tell my friends? Even worse, how was I going to tell my parents? What was going to happen to my body? I was angry with God. How could He let this happen to me? I knew I had sinned…but so does everyone. It's not like I slept around like some of the girls I knew. I was smart. I was careful. So why me?

I was most scared about telling my parents. I didn't want to see them disappointed, or worse, disown me. I was eight weeks pregnant before I got up the courage to tell my dad. He was sitting in his recliner watching television, and my mom was speaking at a women's retreat at our church. I walked into the living room, climbed into my dad's lap, and started to cry. He asked me if I was okay. When I didn't answer, he asked if I was pregnant. I couldn't even speak. I just nodded. We didn't say anything after that. We just rocked and cried until my mom came home. I couldn't even look her in the eye, so my dad gave her the news while I was still in the room. I think she was so shocked that she didn't even shed a tear.

I didn't attend church the night my dad told our congregation. I was too ashamed. I've been told he read a prepared statement from the pulpit and then left the platform. What happened next was remarkable. Instead of condemnation, the members of my youth group left their seats and surrounded my parents and my brothers. They laid their hands on them and prayed. While I was sitting at home ashamed and hopeless, God was already working in my family.

When I was three months pregnant, I left school and was home-schooled. I didn't feel much different except for the occasional morning sickness. I went out with my friends, and I did the normal teenage stuff like going to the mall or the movies. For a time I thought that life might not change very much. Maybe I would be one of those girls who doesn't even realize she's pregnant, and then one day the baby just pops out. Maybe I could just forget about what happened and move on with my life.

That all changed when I felt a tiny little flutter. Was it from my breakfast? It happened again. And again. Did my baby just kick? I placed my hands over my stomach and closed my eyes. I was not alone. There was a tiny person growing inside me. Something happened to me that day. I came to the realization my life no longer revolved around me.

I knew I had to make a decision and do what was best for my child. That much was clear. But what? Abortion was out of the question. I couldn't justify ending an innocent life that had only just begun. But how was I, a 16-year-old without a job and clueless about children, going to raise a baby? I thought about my parents, but I couldn't picture them raising a newborn. That just didn't seem right either.

I got on my knees and prayed for wisdom. I asked God for a clear answer. John 3:16 kept coming to my mind: "God so loved the world that he gave his one and only Son, that whoever believes in him shall not perish but have eternal life." God spoke to my heart: "I gave you My Son. Now it's time for you to give Me yours. I will take care of him and keep him safe. I will give him a family and an abundant life. I will bring peace to your heart and give you hope with a future." I knew what I had to do. I had to give my child to God and to a loving family. Not long after that prayer, I had an ultrasound. The nurse practitioner told me I was going to have a boy. I already knew.

We contacted a social worker from an adoption agency to help us through the process. One day she brought a stack of photo books to my house. Out of all the potential adoptive families, I was supposed to choose my top three. How in the world was I going to choose a family for my child? I thought the biggest decision of my life was supposed to be picking out the color of my prom dress! Now I was making a decision about who would raise and mold my child for the rest of his life. I was numb as I looked through the books.

By the time I reached the last book, I had given up hope. I didn't have a top one, much less a top three. I thought, "Lord, I know this is what You want for my son and me, but I just can't bring myself to give him to any of these families."

Then I opened the last book.

There was a young, attractive couple in their twenties. Due to some physical challenges, they were unable to have children of their own. She was a music teacher, and he owned a local contracting business. They looked different than the rest. They seemed energetic and fun. It wasn't until I flipped to the last page that I knew they were special. On the last page there was an empty picture space framed with a paper heart. On the top of the page it said, "Delight yourself in the LORD, and He will give you the desires of your heart" [Psalm 37:4 NASB]. Underneath the picture, there was a space that said, "For the child of our heart." They had left a space for a child. No other family had done that. God kept His promise. I had found a family for my son.

He was born on a Friday afternoon. I stayed with him for two days before I had to say good-bye. On the last day, I wrapped him in a blanket and sat with him by myself for two hours. When I was pregnant, my doctor told me that he could hear noises and recognize my voice, so I sang songs and played the piano for him. One of my favorite songs as a child was "You Are My Sunshine." As I rocked him during the last moments we would ever see each other, I sang that song.

On that day I began to understand what it meant to give my life completely to the Lord. It wasn't until I held my own child in my arms that I could comprehend the love God has for His children. It wasn't until I said good-bye to my only son that I knew how difficult it must have been for God to send His only Son to save a sinful world. I realized that giving your life to God only starts when you ask Him to come into your heart. Giving my life completely to Him meant fully surrendering my life to His will, trusting Him completely, and committing to His call, no matter how difficult it might be.

I'm almost 30 years old now. I have a wonderful husband and a beautiful daughter. When I look at her, I'm reminded of my son. Most important, I'm reminded that God never gave up on me. He promised He would give me a future and a hope. He did.

Personal Reflections

1. Have you let your past mistakes keep you from living in God's forgiveness? If yes, what will you do about it today?

2. Do you need to ask someone for forgiveness? When will you approach him or her?

3. What practical consequences have you experienced from some of your mistakes? In what ways did those consequences bring you closer to or further from God?

4. If someone you know has made mistakes, is it difficult for you to forgive him or her? How can you reflect God's love by forgiving others?

5. How has God used your mistakes to help you grow? How can you make them part of your testimony to let people know how much God loves them?

THE LABEL TO AVOID

LURE OR PURE?

. . . .

Impression: *The first and immediate effect of an experience or perception upon the mind.*

. . . .

Are you a fan of reality television? Even if you aren't, you've probably caught enough of these shows to realize more drama means bigger ratings. It can get really ugly when the participants are pulled away from the group and interviewed one-on-one. The biting comments about others usually come back to bite the contestants in the end. Do these people not realize that everyone is going to hear their comments when the show is aired, including the people they are cutting down?

While reality television doesn't mirror the reality of relationships, there are some interesting dynamics reflected by reviewing the first impressions of others. How do you size up someone you meet? What catches your immediate attention? It's easy to be flattered by a guy and let that soften your judgment. Have you ever heard these pickup lines?

- "Did it hurt when you fell from heaven? Because I know you must be an angel."

- "What time is it? I just want to remember the exact moment I fell in love with you."

- "Apart from being beautiful, what do you do for a living?"

Even when we know these are "pickup" lines, they might still make us smile and get our hearts beating faster. But seriously, have you considered what people think when they notice you? What sense they get of who you are when they see you? What do you do that grabs people's attention? And can you get the attention of the guy you're interested in?

First impressions or the way you are perceived matters. We've talked a lot about the importance of your inner beauty, but what you wear, how you act toward guys, and the way you communicate all influence how people perceive you.

from Robin...

Perception Is Reality

I'm surprised what some people will write when they're sitting behind their computer screens. Since I work on television as a news anchor every morning, some people feel free to send in their criticism. Sometimes they have valid points, but other times they just come across as mean. And even as a veteran newsperson, it's easy to get my feelings hurt when I open up an e-mail and see a message that reads "you need a haircut" or "you wear too much makeup." It's easy to get down on myself when people share that they don't like the way I look or how I do my job.

On the flip side, there are e-mails that make my day because they are filled with encouragements, such as "you looked great this morning" or "the way you reported on that story made an impact."

Like most of us, I tend to focus on the negative comments. But whether the comments are positive or negative, if I listened without evaluation, my emotions—and probably my hair—would be a mess every day.

God has taught me not to get caught up in the emotional roller coaster of the way people perceive things. Instead, I'm to focus on pleasing Him and living according to His standards. I ask Him to show me how to be the person He wants me to be.

In the news business, a lot is built on perception. I find it humorous that most people I meet in public comment, "Wow! You are so much bigger on TV!" I think they are trying to give me a compliment, but it doesn't always come across that way.

You see, it is true what they say. The camera does add 10 pounds. Also, I'm 5'2" and have a slender build. My coanchor, a guy, is well over six feet tall. When we stand side-by-side, there is a dramatic difference.

To downplay this difference, there are illusions we produce with simple adjustments. For instance, every morning I boost my anchor chair higher than his so we look more even in height on camera. That gives the perception that I'm much taller than I really am. In television, perception is reality.

The same is true in your relationships with guys. Guys get an impression of you based on the clothes you wear. I have a dear friend who has three girls. When she sees her daughters walking out the door, she reminds them, "What are you advertising?" In other words, what they wear is sending a message. For example, if one of her teen daughters wants to wear a low-cut top on a date, my friend asks if she is advertising her breasts because that's what her date is going to notice right away.

Do you think twice about the clothes you pick out each day? What you wear speaks volumes. Here's a good way to think about this. You know what a cowboy looks like by the way he dresses, right? The same can be said for athletes and businesspeople. Even prostitutes advertise by their clothing choices…or lack thereof.

Because guys are especially stimulated by sight, modesty is extremely important if you want to attract a guy who honors God by his standards and behavior. If you wear a low-cut shirt, a super short skirt, or other provocative clothing, you are essentially emphasizing your sexuality, which not only sends the wrong message but can stimulate the guy and cause him to struggle with sexual thoughts and lust.

Stimulate means "to arouse, excite, or even turn on." If you're wearing a top that shows cleavage (the size of your breasts) or a skirt that is so short that you can't bend over, you can bet the guy you're talking to or who is watching you isn't looking at your eyes. He's not connecting to you as a person—he's connecting to your body.

First Samuel 16:7 says, "People look at the outward appearance, but the LORD looks at the heart." The message of modesty begins in your heart. When you know you have Jesus as your Lord and Savior and He lives in your heart, that will affect your clothing choices. Think of it as opportunities to let people know you love and honor Jesus. When you dress modestly, people notice. And your clothing choices are backing up your Christian witness and demeanor.

What messages are you sending?

To Lure or to Be Pure

"Lure" or "pure"? These two words are only one letter different, but their meanings are worlds apart. To lure or to be pure? To answer this question there are two related issues to focus on. The first regards modesty. The second relates to pursuing boys.

The reason we think these are connected is because sometimes outward appearance is directly related to getting a guy's attention. Too often girls who want boyfriends take shortcuts. Instead of concentrating on letting boys see their inner qualities, which can be a slow process, they want to gain instant attention by wearing clothing that essentially advertises their sexual attributes.

We could get into a huge debate on "what's appropriate" and "what's not appropriate" when it comes to clothes, but that can be subjective and make people defensive, frustrated, and even angry. Modesty standards have been different in every generation. Fifty years ago, girls weren't allowed to wear pants to school or almost anywhere else! A hundred years ago, women who didn't wear ankle-length dresses were frowned upon.

What's important to consider when you're choosing what to wear is what you're saying by your clothes. Are you trying to impress others with who *you* are or *who you are in Christ*? In other words, are you advertising yourself as an ambassador of Christ? Galatians 1:10 says, "Am I now trying to win the approval of human beings, or of God? Or am I trying to please people? If I were still trying to please people, I would not be a servant of Christ." Pleasing God is the heart issue. He cares more about your inward attitude than your outward appearance. He wants you to draw attention to Him instead of to yourself.

Does that mean God doesn't care about what you wear? Absolutely not. The apostle Paul wrote, "I also want the women to dress modestly, with decency and propriety, adorning themselves, not with elaborate hairstyles or gold or pearls or expensive clothes, but with good deeds, appropriate for women who profess to worship God" (1 Timothy 2:9-10). Does this mean you can't fix your hair or wear nice clothes? Not exactly. What Paul is saying is your identity should not be wrapped up in your outward appearance. Consider how much time and money you spend shopping for clothes and accessories. Do you buy out of need or a constant desire to impress others? Are you more concerned about purchasing items for yourself or do you have a heart to give to others?

So what should you wear? It may seem strange, but consider asking your parents about your outfit. We're sure they'll be glad to share their opinions. Also, make sure you follow the dress code at school. Here are some more tips to help you out.

Wear clothing that fits. It's natural for your body to change, and you will most likely gain weight and grow taller. Take inventory of your closet and get rid of the things that are too tight.

Buy a full-length mirror. Check both the front and back before you head out. Wondering about the cut of your shirt? Bend over in front of the mirror to double-check how much is revealed. If you're wearing a dress or shorts, check your backside when you're bent over. Does it come up too high in the back? You'd be surprised at how often you bend or lean over during the day…when you're studying, if you drop something, and so on.

Undergarments should stay undergarments. If your bra straps are showing on your shoulders or your panties show above your jeans or below your shorts, consider the message guys are getting. Revealing the color of your bra or panties to your guy friends tempts them to want to see more.

The way you dress can affect your confidence. If you're giving a presentation at school, if you're trying out for a part in the school musical, or if you're going on a date, wearing your best or knowing you look good boosts your confidence. This can even carry over to important events, such as major tests at school, college entrance exams, and job interviews.

Ask your dad or an adult you trust for his opinion. If you really want to pass the modesty test, "pass by your dad" on the way out the door. Sometimes moms say, "That's so cute!" while dads are saying, "Whoa! Wait a minute." Believe it or not, your dad was once a teen boy, and he knows what is and isn't appropriate when it comes to provocative apparel. If you really want brutal honesty, take your dad with you when you shop for clothes. Dads can be good modesty screeners.

Consider your spiritual brothers. Over and over again, we've heard guys say, "I wish girls knew how difficult they make it on guys by what they wear." A guy who wants to follow Christ can use your help in the area of keeping his thoughts pure. Are you helping out your brother in Christ or are you causing him to stumble? And if you are starting to spend more time with a guy, make sure you are consistently aware of being modest in your clothing choices. Modest doesn't mean boring. Show your personality, just don't show everything else.

Piercings and tattoos. When it comes to tattoos, remember that they are essentially permanent and will be part of you the rest of your life. What may seem cool today might be out in a few years. We're not out to be legalistic, but we want you to think about this. What's acceptable to some is not acceptable to others. Paul said, "'I have the right to do anything,' you say—but not everything is beneficial. 'I have the right to do anything'—but not everything is constructive. No one should seek their own good, but the good of others" (1 Corinthians 10:23-24). We're not making a judgment call on whether tattoos and piercings are right or wrong. Just consider what they say about your walk with Christ. Will these adornments hurt your testimony or help it? You should also consider your future. What careers are you considering? What impression or message will certain tattoos or piercings give to prospective employers? Many employers have standards regarding appearance, so carefully consider how your future might be affected by your choice to get tattooed or pierced, by the type you have done if you choose to do it, and by the location.

The Character You Want to Wear

The New Testament contains several passages addressing the issue of holy living, and some of the passages relate specifically to modesty and purity. But overall, God is most concerned about the inner qualities you are developing. The more you focus on your inner character, the easier it will be to make decisions that honor God when it comes to what is appropriate regarding clothing choices.

Keep in mind that prior to Christ's coming and the indwelling of the Holy Spirit, those who sought to follow God were under the Old Testament laws. When Christ came and offered grace through faith, there was freedom from the law. In addition, the gospel was spreading throughout the region and was offered to Jews and Gentiles. For Gentile believers, standards for holiness weren't always the same, especially when it came to the food they ate and circumcision. These were huge issues back in the first century, so the writers of the New Testament addressed many of them.

The apostle Paul wrote several passages encouraging Christ followers to understand how grace covers sin, but that grace doesn't give believers an excuse to continue in sin. He wrote to the Roman believers, "Now that you have been set free from sin and have become slaves of God, the benefit you reap leads to holiness, and the result is eternal life" (Romans 6:22).

One of our favorite passages about God's standards for living is found in Paul's letter to the Colossians. You might say it's God's version of the show *What Not to Wear*. Just like the popular television makeover series, there are things that should be thrown in the trash and replaced with new. For a moment, think of Paul as your personal consultant as you read the following spiritual fashion advice.

Get rid of the old. "But now you must also *rid yourselves* of all such things as these: anger, rage, malice, slander, and filthy language from your lips. Do not lie to each other, since you have *taken off your old self* with its practices and have put on the new self" (Colossians 3:8-10).

What to put on. "As God's chosen people, holy and dearly loved, *clothe yourselves* with compassion, kindness, humility, gentleness and patience. Bear with each other and forgive one another if any of you has a grievance against someone. Forgive as the Lord forgave you. And over all these virtues put on love, which binds them all together in perfect unity" (verses 12-14).

Remove anger and replace it with compassion. Remove the desire to be a "mean girl" and replace it with humility and kindness. Remove the thirst for revenge and replace it with forgiveness. And the accessory that beats the latest purse or belt? *Love.* Why? Because it gives the final statement of unity.

Do you want to attract a godly guy? Focus on your character wardrobe. It will always be a good fit and look great!

from Lauren...

Patience v. Pursuer

When I was growing up, my mom gave me strict rules about calling boys. "You don't call boys," she said. "Wait for them to call you." She knew the importance of boys pursuing the relationship instead of it being the other way around.

This happened even when I met Randy. My friend Sherry gave me Randy's number. I told her I didn't call boys, and he would have to call me first. I usually followed my mom's instructions because they were her rules, but over time I learned there are good reasons for letting the guy do the calling. By letting Randy call me instead of the other way around, it allowed him to take the role of leader in the relationship. God has a specific design for guy/girl relationships, and He made guys and girls different so each could fill their respective specific roles. When God created Adam, He made Adam the hunter, provider, and leader. When God created Eve, she was given the roles of helpmate and supporter. Following these roles is important in creating strong guy/girl relationships.

As I work with teen girls across the country, I see a lot of girls who disregard this simple principle. They are becoming the "pursuers" in the relationships. Some of the Facebook posts I see are alarming. And I'm very aware of the text messages that are even more provocative. I'm seeing a pattern of girls initiating dating relationships, picking fights with other girls over a guy, and even instigating physical relationships. Girls are becoming aggressive, and there's nothing attractive about it. While there may be cougars who chase after younger men, there's a new generation of cougar cubs who have an appetite for guys.

I'm not saying you can't have guy friends you call. But there's a difference between calling your guy friend to talk about math class and calling a guy to initiate a romantic relationship. God's Word is clear about the roles of men and women in relationships. Ephesians 5:22-23 says, "Wives, submit yourselves to your own husbands as you do to the Lord. For the husband is the head of the wife as Christ is the head of the church, his body, of which he is the Savior." Even though this passage is talking about married couples, we can take a cue from it for our dating relationships as well. God made women to be responders, and He made men to be leaders. "Submission" is a word that makes some girls and women cringe. But submission isn't about control or who is bossing whom. It is about respect and order.

The best example of submission is Jesus in the garden of Gethsemane. On the night He was betrayed, He prayed, "My Father, if it is possible, may this cup be taken from me" (Matthew 26:39). But in the ultimate act of submission, Jesus affirmed, "Yet not as I will, but as you will." When we submit to the Lord's leading, we also submit to His design for guy/girl relationships, thus allowing ourselves to be pursued instead of becoming the pursuers.

As I've observed this pursuit behavior among teen girls, I've asked why this is happening. I know I haven't always adhered to my mom's rule. I've thought back to the times when I've sent the first text or called a guy first. I think my attitude can be summed up in one word: impatience. Impatience rushes in when we think our plans are better than God's or when we don't want to wait on His timing. Impatience breeds aggression and causes us to be in a position to mess up God's best plan.

The opposite of impatience is waiting. Psalm 130:5 says, "I wait for the LORD, my whole being waits, and in his word I put my hope." Patience means trusting God's plan is better than your own. It means His timing in your life is perfect. The second part of that verse says your hope can be found in God's Word. Why? Because God is not a liar, so every promise in His Word is true. You can take that to the bank!

So the next time you are tempted to take matters into your own hands and post that Facebook status or hit the send button on that text message, think about whether your message shows patience or pursuit. Consider God's promise in Isaiah 40:31: "Those who hope in the LORD will renew their strength." Remember, your hope is in the Lord, in His timing, and in His Word.

Delilah

The book of Judges should carry a PG-13 warning label. And some of the chapters should probably say "For mature audiences only." The story of Samson and Delilah is quite racy.

Samson's life contains all the elements of a superhero tale. God empowered him with supernatural strength as long as he kept the Nazirite vow of not cutting his hair. These instructions were given to Samson's mother by an angel of the Lord:

> Now see to it that you drink no wine or other fermented drink and that you do not eat anything unclean. You will become pregnant and have a son whose head is never to be touched by a razor because the boy is to be a Nazirite dedicated to God from the womb. He will take the lead in

delivering Israel from the hands of the Philistines (Judges 13:4-5).

Although Manoah and his wife had received divine instructions on raising their son, they surely had no idea that Samson would possess incredible brute strength.

Although Samson grew up and kept the vow to leave his hair untouched, he wasn't as careful with the other parts of the vow involved in being a Nazirite. These included not drinking wine or being around dead bodies (Numbers 6:2-6). While there's no indication that Samson drank from the vine, he didn't avoid being around vineyards (Judges 14:5). And Samson definitely created a lot of carnage in his escapades.

Through riddles, revenge, and a renegade spirit, Samson killed many Philistines. He was a much-wanted man in the eyes of his enemies, especially the Philistines. When they couldn't bring him down, they turned to the wiles and ways of a woman—Delilah. Samson fell in love with Delilah, but we're not told if she loved him back (Judges 16:4). When the Philistine rulers offered Delilah a hefty sum of money in exchange for Samson's super-strength secret, she agreed to use her feminine wiles to discover the secret to Samson's strength.

Samson, a man who loved riddles, played along with Delilah when she asked him the source of his strength. First he tells her that if he is tied up with seven fresh leather strips he couldn't get free. So while he is sleeping, Delilah ties him up. She then tests him by waking him and saying the Philistines were coming. Samson instantly breaks the bonds.

Delilah persists. And of course she would! She wanted her reward and was determined to get it. Samson tricks her two more times—once telling her to tie him up with ropes and then tying the braids of his hair into the fabric of a loom.

When none of these tactics worked, Delilah resorts to her final strategy—nagging: "It came about when she pressed him daily with her words and urged him, that his soul was annoyed to death" (Judges 16:16 NASB). She wore him down. After Samson reveals his heart and the secret of his strength, Delilah lulls the strongman to sleep and calls in someone to do the dirty work—to shave off his hair.

What happens next isn't pretty. Samson's strength leaves, the Philistines take him prisoner and gouge out his eyes. They didn't want to give him a quick death, just slow torture.

At this point of the story, we never hear about Delilah again. We can only ponder what happened. Did she take the money and run? Did she feel remorse? While we won't know these answers until we get to heaven, there are definitely some lessons we can learn from this flirtatious woman.

First, God has given women the ability to attract men, whether for good or bad. How are you going to attract guys? Will it be through godly character or through your body? Proverbs 7:21-22 warns guys about this type of woman: "With persuasive words she led him astray; she seduced him with her smooth talk. All at once he followed her like an ox going to the slaughter." What about you? Are you a flirt who likes to tease guys and make them think you're interested? If attracting guys is a game to you, then reevaluate your motives. Many of the boys we interviewed told us that it is very confusing to date because many girls lead them on.

Second, Delilah's motive for continuing the relationship wasn't in Samson's best interest. No, it was for her own wealth—the bribe money. Do you want a relationship for selfish reasons or do you think about the heart and interest of the guy you like? Philippians 2:3-4 says, "In humility value others above yourselves, not looking to your own interests but each of you to the interests of others." We see this many times when girls aggressively pursue guys only because they are showing interest in other girls. Jealousy is involved. Instead of really caring about the guys, the girls play games. They think, "If I can't have him, I'll make sure another girl can't either." There can be tough competition in relationships.

Finally, the best way to attract a godly guy is by modeling godliness. Proverbs 31:30 reminds us, "Charm is deceptive, and beauty is fleeting; but a woman who fears the LORD is to be praised."

Simple Ways to Help Your Guy

Hopefully you're not searching for a guy's weaknesses so you can exploit them. No, we pray that you will look for ways to help him, to support him. There are lots of things you can do to help out your guy friends. Here are several simple things that will help your guy friends keep from stumbling and also keep you from inadvertently leading them on.

- When sitting, especially in a skirt or short shorts, make sure to keep your legs together.

- Make clothing choices that don't reveal cleavage or cracks. We heard this over and over from guys.

- You may think it's playful to put your hand on a guy's leg when sitting next to him. This easily arouses him. If you know this and still do it, you are compromising your purity as much as his.

- When you are doing something recreational, such as swimming or playing a physical game, pay attention to physical contact. When you wrap your legs around a guy or sit on his shoulders when playing pool volleyball, it's really hard for a guy not to be stimulated. Use good judgment.

- Hug sideways only. Face-to-face contact is much more intimate. Several guys mentioned to us that if you're just friends, keep the hugs on a side-to-side basis. This also includes hugging adult men, such as a youth minister or pastor.

- Keep your physical, mental, and emotional boundaries. Texting your youth leader if he is male is not appropriate unless it's to ask a simple question. Texting just to say "hi" is not okay. If you feel uncomfortable around an adult male, talk to a female adult who will help you handle the situation or take appropriate measures.

Personal Reflections

1. What did you wear to school today? What messages do you think you sent?

2. How do you think guys perceive you based on your outward appearance, especially what you wear?

3. How can your outward appearance reflect God's standard for holiness?

4. Are you always the first to call or text message a guy? If so, why do you think you do that?

5. "Clothe yourselves with compassion, kindness, humility, gentleness and patience. Bear with each other and forgive one another if any of you has a grievance against someone" (Colossians 3:12-14). What character qualities do you need to trash and which ones do you need to put on? How can you do that practically this week?

6. Are you going to let guys pursue you instead of you pursuing them? How will you implement this decision?

7. Consider Delilah. What was wrong with her motives? What did you learn from her that will help you in relating to guys?

REALITY TV DATING
v. REAL-LIFE DATING
THE MEDIA'S INFLUENCE

Reality: *Based on fact, observation, or experience and so undisputed; used to emphasize the accuracy or appropriateness of a particular thing.*

T he impact of media today can be a positive influence, but on the flip side the message the media sends can also pack a negative punch.

from Robin...
When Television Involves Tragedy

April 19; 9:02 a.m.

It was a picture-perfect day in Oklahoma. The redbud trees were in bloom, the sun was shining, and spring was in the air.

The year was 1995. Bill Clinton was president of the United States. The number one song was "This Is How We Do It" by Montell Jordan, and the movie *Toy Story* was just a few months from being released.

If you were alive, you were probably just crawling. Most of you weren't even born. For me, it was a day of excitement as I began a new phase of my career and took advantage of a television news reporting opportunity that had come my way. Life on this April day seemed as normal as could be in the heartland of America.

And then it happened.

A 5,000-pound fertilizer bomb was detonated in front of the Alfred P. Murrah Federal Building in downtown Oklahoma City. On that day, a nine-story building became a war zone; 168 people lost their lives, including 19 children under the age of 6.

I was in a meeting at our television station, located about 10 miles north of the downtown area. People from miles around heard what sounded like a sonic boom, including me. Little did we know that within hours we would be telling the story of a terrorist attack in the city I call home.

The aftermath chaos unfolded on every media outlet. My assignment was reporting live less than one block from the attack. I saw things that day no one should witness in her lifetime. In the midst of pandemonium, we were told to quickly evacuate because there was the threat of a second bomb. As I pitched the report back to the anchors at the station, I silently prayed for protection. Thankfully, there was no second bomb.

Families of people who worked at or were in the Federal Building gathered at the First Christian Church in Oklahoma City that evening, where I was continuing to report live. They were all trying to find out one thing—the fate of their loved ones. Person after person begged me to show their family member's picture on TV in hopes that someone had seen them alive or at a local hospital. It was an agonizing evening for everyone. Things like this don't happen in the middle of America— or so we'd thought.

from Lauren...
When Television Becomes Trash

Reality television shows are everywhere. Whether it's *Survivor* or *Keeping Up with the Kardashians,* reality television is on almost every channel. There are some shows with positive messages, such as *Extreme Home Makeover,* which builds or remodels houses for people who need help, but for the most part reality shows have little to do with real life.

I got a little taste of being on a reality show during my year as Miss America. The Learning Channel Network (TLC) had just bought the rights to airing the pageant. To promote the upcoming contest, I was picked for a makeover on a mini-episode of the show *What Not to Wear.* The premise was for Stacy and Clinton, the hosts, to recreate me from an "Over-the-top Pageant Patty" to a more glamorous "me." To show a dramatic before and after, extensions were placed in my hair that went all the way down my back. My face was painted with more makeup than I've ever worn in my life. They created an illusion that the "before" picture was what I looked like when I won the crown and the "after" was what I should look like.

I had a big problem with the whole premise because it was all a lie, a sham. It made me feel worse about myself, not better. But that's what reality television does. It gives the people involved and viewers a warped view of everyone. It can also skew our expectations of love and relationships.

There's no better picture of distorted relationships in reality TV than the ever-popular "relationship" reality shows. There we sit, surrounded by our girlfriends, waiting with a bowl of popcorn in one hand and M&Ms in the other, watching the drama unfold. The music begins and a handsome bachelor looks into the distance with only one question on his mind: "Which woman is my 'true' love?"

We watch as the women are whisked away in helicopters to romantic destinations and over-the-top dates. (And why does there always seem to be a hot tub involved?) It's easy to wish we were the women being pursued. Real life and dating seem so boring! Reality shows glamorize casual sex and justify letting our morals lapse or even disappear.

The problem is that reality television many times causes us to compare it with our lives. Our expectations of relationships become unrealistic. Comparison breeds disappointment and robs people of joy.

A Powerful Message

Do you believe you're not influenced by television or other media? Think again. By the time you turn 18, if you're a typical television viewer, you've seen around 350,000 commercials. No doubt, this form of entertainment has influenced you. And you're surrounded by all kinds of media throwing messages at you. And you multitask to take in several forms of information at once. For instance, you read a magazine, watch TV, keep up with your Facebook, and follow your Twitter feed on your phone all at the same time.

Information gathered by the Teen Futures Media Network of the University of Washington's College of Education revealed that the average teenager spends more time watching television than any other activity besides sleeping (that includes spending time at school). Viewing habits increase in preteen years and decline after the age of 21. The average American teen spends about 20 hours a week watching television, with the heaviest viewers coming from low-income households.[1]

To Conform or Reform?

The entire subject of how you deal with the media, in all its forms, boils down to how you choose to respond to the culture of the world. Unless you plan on never having contact with the outside world, you are going to need to discover God's standards and learn how to apply them to what you take in via media. Here are a few verses from God's Word to give you a quick look at His perspective.

- *Colossians 2:8:* "See to it that no one takes you captive through hollow and deceptive philosophy, which depends on human tradition and the elemental spiritual forces of this world rather than on Christ."

- *Romans 12:2:* "Do not conform to the pattern of this world, but be transformed by the renewing of your mind. Then you will be able to test and approve what God's will is—his good, pleasing and perfect will."

- *James 4:4:* "Anyone who chooses to be a friend of the world becomes an enemy of God."

- *1 Peter 2:11:* "Dear friends, I urge you, as foreigners and exiles, to abstain from sinful desires, which wage war against your soul."

- *1 John 2:15:* "Do not love the world or anything in the world. If anyone loves the world, love for the Father is not in them."

These verses show that if you live your life to meet the world's standards, you will find disappointment and be led on a path that pulls you away from the Lord. Are you wondering how this is important to your dating life? What does media influence have to do with guy relationships? Actually, the media heavily influences your views on dating, marriage, and sexuality. Your interaction with the opposite sex is also intertwined with how you interact using technology. Digital communication has almost deleted the need for face-to-face interaction in many instances. And how can you truly know someone if the majority of your conversations occur through text messages, which lack the subtle clues we depend on to discern what is true and what is false?

Let's look at some things to think about before attempting to navigate through the influences of mass media.

Social Media

If you pick up a book on relationships written 10 years ago, you won't find social media mentioned. Facebook and Twitter weren't even invented! You probably have never known life without it. While it's fun to keep up with what your friends are doing, there are some challenges and things to consider before diving into the world of social networking.

Be careful about the photos you post and the language you use. You had a great time at the slumber party with all your girlfriends. Silly smiles and pranks are fun to post. But what about the pajamas you were wearing? You might think it's innocent, but the cami you wore with your short pj bottoms might not be suitable for public viewing. Think even more about the friends you may be tagging in the photo. Are they dressed appropriately? Are any of you in a compromising position? The images on the Internet leave permanent marks that can't be erased. A comment trail based on an inappropriate comment can follow you for a long time—even when you look for a job! Check your privacy settings and consider whether anyone or just your "friends" can see the photos you post.

Are you posting "I love you" to a certain guy on a social networking site? In six months, when the relationship might be over, how are you going to get rid of it? Once something is on the web, it's there forever…somewhere.

A good test: Each time you post a status update or upload an image, do the "Grandma" test. Would you be embarrassed if your grandma saw what you are about to post?

Consider the feelings of others when you post something about someone else. The tragedy and outcome of cyber-bullying online has escalated in the past few years, and the results have been devastating. Suicides of some teens have caused parents to look at legal ramifications and criminal charges for those who have instigated the bullying. If you are the target of cyber-bullying, don't keep it a secret. It's important to tell your parents or authorities quickly. And if you know someone who is being negatively affected by cyber-bullying, talk to her…and mention it to an adult so everyone stays safe.

If someone wants to be your "friend" on social networking and you don't know him or her well or at all, it's OK to "ignore" the request. Sexual predators have a track record of targeting teens and preteens on the Internet. Social networking is the easiest way for them to get into your life and sound like they're nice. Never begin a conversation with someone you don't know through social networking sites. Protect your profile, and be extremely careful in what you post. Never give out personal information that could lead someone to you, your house, your friends, or your friends' houses. Don't post information that reveals when no one will be at home or when you'll be home alone.

How much time do you spend on social networking sites? It's easier than ever to spend lots of time online now that it can be accessed via smart phones and tablets. How many times do you look at a social network site during the day? How much time are you spending in God's Word? Compare the two, and you might realize some of your time could be spent in a more productive way.

Is there drama online? Don't play out your personal drama with others on Twitter, Facebook, or other media forms. Some conversations should only be handled face-to-face. Everything you say online is a public postcard for the world to see. "Let your conversation be always full of grace, seasoned with salt, so that you may know how to answer everyone" (Colossians 4:6).

Worldwide Web

There are more issues to consider regarding how you spend time online. There's a song for preschoolers entitled "O Be Careful, Little Eyes." The lyrics emphasize that what you see, hear, do, and say, and where you go matters because the Lord is watching with love from above. This is an important principle for all ages, especially when addressing issues on the Internet. Whether it's a video gone viral or pornography, there are a lot of things to avoid when browsing the worldwide web.

Pornography used to be seen primarily as a guy issue, but pornography for girls and women is becoming an increasing problem. Don't fall into a trap of watching inappropriate videos or pictures that could lead to shame, addiction, and heartache. The effects of pornography have destroyed many relationships, including marriages.

Jesus spoke many times about Christians being light in the midst of darkness. He specifically talks about the importance of what our eyes reveal: "Your eye is the lamp of your body. When your eyes are healthy, your whole body also is full of light. But when they are unhealthy, your body also is full of darkness" (Luke 11:34).

Phones and Texting

Consider what you text. Would you want that photo or comment forwarded to your entire school? Probably not, *but it happens all the time.* If you've contemplated sending a guy a flirty message or provocative photo, don't be surprised if it backfires. Many girls have walked down the halls of school with their reputations tattered because of a message or photo they would gladly take back if they could.

Breaking up via text message? Not a good idea, and certainly not a kind and personal approach. If you're ready to end a relationship with a guy, respect him enough to talk to him face-to-face. You'll most likely handle the conversation with more sensitivity—something you'll appreciate if you're ever on the other end of a breakup.

Television and Movies

Almost every television show or movie rated PG or above contains sexual content or innuendos. Whether you realize it or not, the more you watch this type of programming, the more your mind becomes desensitized to sexual situations. In other words, the more you watch and hear that premarital sex is normal and even appropriate, the easier it will be for you to compromise on God's standards. If you feel uncomfortable seeing two people making out in public, why would you watch it on television? And remember, television isn't real life. The consequences of jumping into bed and other sins are seldom revealed.

Set boundaries for what you will and won't watch. And if a movie crosses the line, walk out of the theater and ask for a refund. Better yet, review movies online and investigate what's included before you agree to go.

Magazines

The erosion of self-image that occurs when a girl flips through magazines full of airbrushed-to-perfection models is real. If you spend time comparing your life and your looks to celebrities and models, you will never find contentment. Wanting what other people have is called "coveting" in the Bible. Remember, God cares about your spiritual growth, not your material possessions accumulation or what you look like.

Do you read magazines to learn about all the celebrity gossip? That's a problem in our culture. "Rumors are dainty morsels that sink deep into one's heart" (Proverbs 18:8 NLT). Girls read stories about people they will never meet. Think about it. How much do you know about Taylor Swift or Justin Bieber's latest album or relationship? Do you personally know Taylor or the Biebs? Our guess is no. So why are you obsessing over them? That's not only celebrity worship, but it can easily cross over to idol worship.

Music

A catchy tune and a good rhythm—the songs you listen to can also be a reflection of what your heart is like. If you're constantly filling your mind with music that demeans women or contains objectionable lyrics, it will eventually influence your tolerance to those subjects. But the opposite is also true. If you fill your mind with music that contains praises to the Lord and lifts up the name of Christ, your life will be positively influenced. Many of the praise songs we love come directly from the pages of Scripture. If you want to invade your mind with God's Word, fill it with music that honors Him. Philippians 4:8 says, "Whatever is true, whatever is noble, whatever is right, whatever is pure, whatever is lovely, whatever is admirable—if anything is excellent or praiseworthy—think about such things."

A Technology Time-out?

We challenge you to a media fast. What is a "fast"? It's choosing a specific period of time to refrain from something that distracts you from spending time with the Lord. A fast is abstaining from one thing and replacing it with a focus on spiritual things. So here's what we want you to consider. Pick one day of the week and decide to abstain from all types of media. Fast from television. Fast from social networking. Fast from texting your friends. Fast from the Internet. Fast from your tablet. It will be hard, but can you do it? We're not asking you to be legalistic about it, but we are encouraging you to consider the challenge and try it out. This will help you realize the extent of your media participation.

The other challenge we'd like you to consider is to write down how much time you spend engrossed in media for a week. You will probably be surprised by how much time you spend using technology. It may open your eyes to realizing you need to add spending more time with God and people face-to-face.

MEDIA CHART

	SUN	MON	TUES	WED	THUR	FRI	SAT
Social Networking							
Texting							
Television							
Movies							
Internet							
Magazines							
Books							
Music							
TOTAL							

The Best Text Message Ever

The best text message you will ever receive is a love letter from God. And He's written to you already! It's called the Bible. God has written His messages of love, forgiveness, grace, and wisdom to you, and He wants to be an intimate part of your daily life. If you forgot your cell phone when you left your home, would you feel lost without it? Would you take the time to turn around to go back and get it? Do you feel the same way about God's Word? Do you feel lost without it? Do you carry it around in your heart everywhere you go? God wants a constant connection with you, and He is waiting for you to connect with Him. If you don't have a Bible app on your phone or tablet, why not get one? That way you can access God's wisdom everywhere you go!

Personal Reflections

1. How has the media influenced your perceptions of what a romantic relationship should look like?

2. How have these perceptions stacked up in real life? How do they compare to God's standards for romantic relationships?

3. What are your media viewing habits? Do you watch inappropriate programs or presentations? Are you tempted to do that when you're alone? Who can you ask to help you set and keep boundaries in this area?

4. Were you challenged by the contents of this chapter? What life changes and decisions are you considering?

5. Is it easier to conform to the world's standards or be reformed by God's Word? What steps can you take to follow God's lead instead of media messages based on the world's standards?

6. Review your Facebook and other social media settings and content. Do you need to make some changes? Do you need to delete some photos or comments?

THE ONE MAN WHO WILL
NEVER LET YOU DOWN

What an incredible blessing it has been to share our hearts with you. There's nothing we want more than to see the next generation of young women fall in love with God and follow Him. We also have a great desire to see you discover God's best in the area of your relationships with guys and patiently wait on His timing. Our prayer is that you will experience and model healthy and godly dating standards and eventually have marriages centered on Christ.

Our Most Important Message to You

A lot of people begin reading a book and never make it to the final chapter. For us, this *is* the most important chapter. In fact, if you just skimmed the book and turned to this page, we pray you'll take the time to read what we have to say. Why? Because if you don't have a relationship with Christ, this is your opportunity to begin a brand-new life with Him.

Your life is a lot like this book. It's a story, and you are part of a bigger story that God has written for all humanity. You are an extremely important part of God's plan. Is your life like a comedy, full of fun moments and sweet reminders of God's visible working hand? If so, that's awesome. But we also know that some lives are laced with tragedies, mistakes, and even situations you didn't choose or couldn't control.

No matter where you are in your story, you have the opportunity to turn the page and start fresh. You have a life story written purposefully by God, but the ending is up to you. You can either acknowledge God as Creator of this world and your Savior now and through eternity or you can muddle through life without Him now and forever. Do you want to begin a new chapter with God? He is waiting for you to accept His invitation and jump into a new life with Him.

The Perfect Guy Is Pursuing You

While there is no perfect human, there is a perfect God who revealed Himself in the form of a man. When sin entered the world, God set in motion a plan that was formed long before creation. He sent His only Son, Jesus, to come to earth as a humble baby. The Bible tells us that Jesus lived a sinless life because He was not just a man, but also God. Jesus offered Himself as the perfect sacrifice for all of our sins by dying on a cross in our place. He conquered death when He arose three days later. He appeared to the disciples and many others before He ascended to heaven, where He now sits at the right hand of God. He has promised that He will return and gather His bride—"the church," consisting of people who believe in Him—to be in His presence forever.

Most girls we know have a common desire: They want to be pursued. There is nothing more romantic than a guy who spends all his energy pursuing the girl he loves. Guess what? There is a perfect guy—and He is pursuing you! His name is Jesus, and He is pursuing you every single day. And when you accept Him as your Lord and Savior, you can be confident that He will always be with you…even on those days when you feel lonely or rejected. Can we share our personal, spiritual love stories with you?

from Lauren...
Who God Is to Me

When I finally understood how I could rely on God for any need, any desire, and any situation in my life, I experienced freedom. While I can't say I have life all figured out, I can say that every day is a journey toward relying on God more and more. God is bigger, stronger, and greater than you and I can ever imagine.

There are more than 100 names for God in the Bible that describe His character. I want to share some of the ones that have been extremely meaningful to me. Look through these names and circle the ones that speak the most to you right now.

- *Jehovah-Yahweh: The Lord Is Our Salvation.* This is foundational to faith in God. God loved you enough to send His Son to die for you. His salvation is offered to everyone as a free gift. Will you receive His gift today?

- *Jehovah-Rohi: The Lord Is Our Shepherd.* A shepherd guides and protects his flock. God wants to be your Shepherd. He wants to be your guide and protector.

- *Jehovah-Shammah: The Lord Who Is Present.* Do you feel lonely? You are never alone because God is always with you. And when you accept Jesus, His presence will become very real to you. He will stand with you during good times and bad. You can take comfort in His presence.

- *Jehovah-Rapha: The Lord Is Our Healer.* Whether you need physical, emotional, or spiritual healing, God will be your Healer. Do you have past hurts that still feel like open wounds? God will help you with those too.

- *Jehovah-Tsidkenu: The Lord Is Our Righteousness.* Because Christ died for you, your sin is wiped out by His loving sacrifice. When God looks at you, instead of seeing the filth of your sin, He sees the blood of Christ. You are right before God through Jesus.

- *Jehovah-Jireh: The Lord Will Provide.* Just like God provided a substitute sacrifice when Abraham was going to offer Isaac as an offering or when God provided an abundance of food to feed 5,000 men with just a few fish and loaves of bread, God will provide for you too.

- *Jehovah-Shalom: The Lord Is Our Peace.* Are you stressed out? Are you doubtful? God will calm your soul in the midst of all the storms you will face in life.

- *El-Roi: The Strong One Who Sees.* Do you long for someone to be totally obsessed with the details of your life? Guess what? God sees you for who you are, and He loves you like crazy!

from Robin...

The Greatest Person I've Ever Met

I've spent more than 60 percent of my life working in television news. It's hard work and long hours. Even during the holidays, the news continues. When people recognize me at the mall or at a restaurant, that's really just icing on the cake. The truth is that it takes years to build credibility and trust with viewers. But after all those years, I still look forward to going to work every day. Why? Because every day is different, and I never know who I'm going to meet or what story I'm going to be covering.

Some of the people I've met are famous. I've been in the company of presidents, governors, superstar athletes, newsmakers, celebrities, and recording artists. One of my favorites was interviewing Oklahoman Garth Brooks during the height of his country music career. It's exciting when I'm going somewhere to interview a "big time star" and get paid while doing it!

But of all the famous people I've had the opportunity to meet, I want to tell you about the greatest person I've ever met. He changed my life in an amazing way, and I've never been the same. I'm talking about Jesus Christ. He gives me love, joy, peace, hope, and, most important, eternal life with Him. Asking Christ into my heart and making Him Lord of my life was the greatest decision I've ever made or ever will make.

If you'd known me before I met Christ, you probably would have thought my life was pretty perfect. I was the main news anchor in Amarillo, Texas. I had the right car, the right clothes, and the right friends. I thought I was better than most people, and I prided myself on not relying on anyone.

But something happened to me one night during a church service. My ego had to be checked at the door. The pastor shared about security in God-reliance versus destruction in self-reliance. I was humbled when I realized that my E-G-O meant "Edging God Out." I realized my life wasn't so great after all. My heart was broken, and I realized my need for a Savior. I began to see clearly how the cross was personal and a gift for me.

The gift Christ offers is available to you too, but it isn't automatic. The Bible says, "All have sinned and fall short of the glory of God" (Romans 3:23). I prayed that night. I confessed my sins and asked God to forgive me. I invited Christ to be my Lord and Savior. I gained assurance that when I die I will live in heaven with Him for eternity.

After all these years of being a Christ follower, I've learned that my personal relationship with Jesus gives me true freedom—freedom that is power from God to do what I can and should do for Him rather than what I want to do for me.

What About You?

Have you made your relationship with Christ personal? Have you confessed your sin and asked Him to forgive you? Have you asked Him to save you and be Lord of your life? It's that simple. If you haven't, the greatest joy we hope for is that you will make the decision to follow Christ right now.

Today is the day you can get real before God. Believing in Christ and what He did on the cross for you is the only thing that can save you from being separated from God. If you're ready to make this decision, the following is a very simple prayer of faith. There are no magic words; only the sincerity of your heart is needed.

> *Dear God, I know I am a sinner, and I need You in my life. Please forgive me of my sins. I confess that You are Lord. I believe in my heart that You came to earth, died on the cross on my behalf, and rose from the grave so that I can live forever with You. I receive Your gift of eternal life and place my trust in You alone. I ask You to come into my heart as my personal Lord and Savior. Thank You. Amen.*

Did you pray that prayer for the first time and really mean it? If so, we want to know, and so will other people. We're so excited for you! If you're going through this book with a group of girls, share your decision with your leader and group. We know they will want to celebrate with you.

We encourage you to find a Bible-believing church that teaches the Word of God. Share with the pastor your decision and follow your decision by getting baptized, as instructed in the Bible. A good minister or youth pastor will walk you through the next steps of your spiritual journey and get you connected with other people who will encourage you and instruct you in your walk with Jesus.

We'd love to hear your story. You can share it by going to our Website: www.withunveiledfaces.com. Click on the "Your Story" link. The best ending to our book will be the beginning of your new life in Christ. We're praying for you!

Personal Reflections

1. After reading the list of names for God Lauren provided, which one spoke to you the most and why?

2. Have you met anyone famous? Why is meeting Christ so much greater than meeting a celebrity?

3. How can a relationship with Christ start a new chapter of your life? If you haven't asked Christ to come into your life, will you do it now?

4. If you already have a relationship with Christ, who in your life doesn't? How will you share your faith with him or her?

5. Spend some time writing out your story of faith in Christ. This is your "testimony." Bring your testimony to your small group and share it.

Please go online to our Website and
share your story with us too.
We want to hear from you!
www.withunveiledfaces.com

SMALL GROUP
LEADER'S GUIDE

For the Girls...

Hi! Even though this section is written for a group leader, if you and your friends are meeting on your own, we're sure you'll find the information helpful as well.

For Small-group Leaders...

Thank you for investing in the lives of young women. While we may never know you personally or have a face-to-face conversation in this life, we know you are a caring, influential woman who desires to see your group of girls grow closer to the Lord. We are hugging you through the pages of this guide and cheering for you through our prayers.

In this leader's guide, we offer a framework for discussions and some ideas and activities to encourage your group to engage on a deeper level. You know your group best, so use this guide in any way that will help you lead. Please feel free to add questions you think are important. Always look for additional ways to get to know your girls better. And at the end of the study, please contact us through our Website at www.withunveiledfaces.com and give us your feedback. We'd love to hear what your experience was like, and we're always looking for better ways to connect with girls and help people who enjoy helping girls grow in Christ.

Remember Paul's words to Timothy, "Guard what has been entrusted to your care" (1 Timothy 6:20). God's Word has been entrusted to you, and so have these girls. We applaud you for taking on this important task.

Robin and Lauren

Chapter 1: The "L" Word

Before your first meeting, have the girls interested in coming sign up and write down their cell phone numbers and addresses. Ask them to get this book and read the introduction and first chapter before the first meeting. A day or two before each meeting, contact the girls and encourage them to come. Remind them to bring *God, Girls, and Guys* and their Bibles to each session.

Because this is your first session, have everyone introduce herself and share something about her life. If your group has never done a study before, don't be surprised if they are hesitant to open up for the first couple of weeks. That's okay. They will warm up over time, and by the end you may have a hard time getting them to be quiet.

Open each session with a brief prayer, asking God to prepare your hearts to hear what He desires to teach you.

Begin this week's discussion by asking three questions:

- "How do you define love?"

- "How does the world define love?"

- "How does God define love?"

Briefly discuss the differences.
Have the girls open their Bibles and read 1 Corinthians 13:4-7.

- "Which of these characteristics of love is hardest to do and why?"

- "Which comes easiest and why?"

Ask the girls to discuss this statement:

- "Relationships are more important than accomplishments."

If your group needs help getting started, ask for some accomplishments, such as getting on a sports team at school. Then compare that accomplishment with the relationships they formed with the team members.

- "Which aspect of being on the team is the most important and why?"

- "Why do girls tend to love storybook endings and finding true love?"

- "Who is your favorite storybook princess, and why do you like her?"

Compare an animated love story with a true love story. Then discuss what unrealistic expectations girls tend to place on relationships, especially girl/guy relationships.

Encourage your group to share real stories of lasting love within their families or friends' families. Some girls may not have great examples in their immediate family, so encourage them to think of other couples who have stayed together.

- "What do you see in those lasting relationships that you would like to see in your future husband and marriage?"

Chapter 2: Mirror, Mirror of My Heart

Materials

- a full-length mirror

- a handheld mirror

- small mirror pieces (from a craft store)

- notebook paper to pass out

- plenty of pens or pencils

Direct the girls to look at themselves in the full-length mirror. Then have them look at their faces in the handheld mirror. And finally have them look at a small part of their faces with a small piece of mirror.

- "Which of the mirrors was easiest to use?"

- "Which was hardest?"

- "What are the differences between the views you saw?"

Discuss how all three items are a reflection of what they look like, but the small piece focuses on something close and personal. It's harder to see a pimple in the full-length mirror, but if the small mirror reflects only a blemish, it becomes all they see.

- "What do you notice about yourself when you quickly glance in a mirror or see a photo of yourself?"

Discuss our tendency to zoom in on a negative aspect rather than a positive one. Ask why they think it's easier to focus on the negative.

Have one of the girls read Psalm 139:13-18.

- "How do these verses change how you see yourself through God's eyes?"

- "Which of these promises spoke to you this week?"

Encourage the girls to consider God's way of looking at them. Remind them that He looks at the heart first. Point out that God sometimes shines His magnifying glass on our blemishes because He wants us to work on certain areas. He does that because He cares about every detail of our lives.

Discuss the difference between caring for your body and being obsessed about appearances.

- "How do you see this difference at school?"

- "What changes do you want to consider making in your life?"

Discuss the book of Esther. Encourage the girls to share their insights.

- "What did you learn from Esther's story?"

Here's a great activity to illustrate God's love and grace for the girls.

- Distribute a blank piece of paper and writing implement to each member.

- Instruct the girls to fold the paper in half lengthwise.

- On one side, ask the group to list "Things I can do that will make God love me more."

- On the back, have them list "Things I can do that will make God love me less."

- After giving them a few moments, ask the girls to open the paper and look at the inside. It's blank! *That is the correct response* to both questions.

Discuss how it feels to know there is nothing they can do that will make God love them less or more.

- "How does God's unconditional love change your view of your value?"

Encourage each girl with a personal comment on one of their inner qualities you see as beautiful.

Close in prayer.

Chapter 3: Evolution of Dating

Materials: index cards and pens

Note to leader: There were many Personal Reflections in this chapter based on the book of Ruth. We encourage you to go through the questions as a group. Ask the girls to think about Ruth's story as if they were Ruth.

- *Read Ruth 1:1.* What do you know about Bethlehem? Why did Elimelech and Naomi move away from there?

- *Read Ruth 1:16.* Why do you think Ruth was so convicted to go back to Bethlehem with Naomi? What does this tell you about Ruth's relationship with God?

- *Read Ruth 2:1.* What do you think it means when Boaz is described as a man of "standing"?

- *Read Ruth 2:9.* What does Boaz's instruction say about the way he protected Ruth physically?

- *Read Ruth 2:15.* What does this verse say about the way Boaz protected Ruth emotionally?

- *Read Ruth 2:22.* What does this verse say about the people we should hang out with?

- *Read Ruth 3:11.* What does this verse say about Ruth's character?

- *Read Ruth 4:14-17.* What do these verses say about God's plan for Ruth's future? How can you trust God with your future relationships?

In the chapter, the girls were challenged to choose a Scripture verse to memorize. Ask the girls if they've done that or are working on it.

Pass out index cards and have the girls write down at least one verse they will commit to memory by the next session. Invite them to be accountable to each other during the week so they'll be ready to recite their verses aloud. Remind the girls to encourage one another and avoid negativity.

Chapter 4: Boy Friends and Boyfriends

Materials: children's building blocks

Divide the group into two teams and have a contest based on who can build the best structure with their blocks. After each team completes the structure, switch the completed projects to the other team with the instruction to tear it apart.

- "Was it easier to build the structure or tear it apart? Which took more time?"

- "Did the structure your team built have more value than the one you tore apart? Why or why not?"

- "Which took more creativity and time—building or destroying?"

Discuss these thoughts regarding building relationships.

- Building friendships takes more time and effort than destroying a friendship.

- Friendships you build over time will have more value than friendships that are "come and go" or based on selfish desires.

Have the girls share some of the characteristics they listed for the different kinds of friends. What are the common themes? Have one or two share some of the qualities they appreciate in their guy friends and why they are important.

Ask the girls to explain why they believe a good boyfriend should also be a good boy friend.

Discuss the five character traits offered as a sample of what God values: honesty, accountability, loyalty, encouragement, and wisdom.

Invite the girls to share what they wrote for question 4 on the "Personal Reflections" page.

When everyone has shared, have the girls stand in a circle. Ask them to hold hands and then ask them to pray silently for the person on their right. Encourage them to pray specifically for their friendships and then thank the Lord for one "builder quality" they see in that person.

Chapter 5: Finding Mr. Right

Materials

- copies of the "Path to Purity Prayer" suitable for hanging or framing

- snacks

Search YouTube for the link to the 1960 commercial for the "Mystery Date" game. Watch it together as a group.

- "How is this commercial humorous?"

- "How is it similar to how we view guys and dating today?"

- "How is it different?"

Ask the girls if they've ever made a list of things they want in a guy relationship. Discuss the pluses and minuses of this (plus: knowing what they value; minus: may keep them from being open to what God has in store for them).

- "Why is it more important to focus on becoming the girl God wants you to be rather than focusing on finding the 'perfect' guy?"

Discuss the sections on justification and sanctification. Be ready to explain the concepts, including why they are so important, if the girls found them difficult to understand.

Have the girls open their Bibles to the book of Hosea.

- "Have you read the story of Hosea and Gomer?"

- "What did you learn from the story?"

- "How is Hosea's love for Gomer similar to God's love for us?"

End this session by passing out copies of the "Path to Purity Prayer" and/or discussing accepting Jesus as Lord and Savior.

Provide snacks to help make the discussion more casual so no one will feel pressured.

Pray out loud for each member of your group. A powerful and meaningful way to do this is to have the girls sit in a circle on the floor or in chairs. You come behind them, place your hands on their shoulders, and pray specifically for each person.

Chapter 6: Tears, Fears, and Drama—Oh My!

Materials

- paper and pens
- toothpaste
- paper plates
- $20 bill

Distribute a blank piece of paper and pen to each person in the group. Ask each girl to draw a picture of herself showing one of the emotions she experienced in the last 24 hours. Have the girls show their pictures so that the others can see which emotion is being portrayed. Allow each girl to share the emotion she experienced and the situation it involved.

Talk about the difference between how girls and guys emotionally respond to situations. For instance, how have they seen guys respond with actions when girls would usually respond with interaction?

Ask the girls to share their results from the Emotional Quotient Quiz. Although there's nothing scientific about it and it is just for fun, what did they learn about themselves? Which questions did they relate to most?

Remind them of the story of Abraham, Sarah, and Hagar. Discuss what they learned about relationships from the story. Also, talk about what they learned about the damage drama can cause.

Discuss gossip. Look at the verses listed, and have the girls select ones to memorize that will help them handle gossip. Discuss solutions to ending gossip and how they can incorporate them into their daily lives.

Lauren talks about the passage in James that describes the tongue as fire. Discuss the damage fire can do when it is out of control.

- "How are your tongues similar?"

Give each girl a tube of toothpaste and a paper plate. Instruct them to empty the contents of the toothpaste as quickly as they can. When they are finished, place a $20 bill in front of them and say, "I'll give you this $20 if you can get all the toothpaste back inside the tube."

Discuss how their words are similar to that toothpaste...once out of their mouth, they can't take them back.

End the session with prayer, praying specifically for the girls to be careful with their emotions and to consider how their words affect people.

Chapter 7: How Far Is Too Far?

Materials: 2 wrapped boxes—one beautiful, the other just a torn or beat-up plastic bag, sack, or box

Show the two gifts to the group. Explain that the beautiful gift is brand-new and has never been opened. It is only to be opened by the person whom it was intended for. Explain that the other gift was at one time new, special, and intended for a specific person. But someone else opened the gift, used it, and then discarded it.

- "How are these gifts like our physical boundaries around sex?"

- "How is keeping yourself pure for your future husband similar to a gift that has been unopened?"

- "What do you think about the gift that was opened and discarded?"

Discuss Lauren's story about setting "a line before a line." Talk about how the girls can establish this standard, and also how they might share their decision with the guys they date.

Discuss the 12 steps of physical progression.

- "Have you considered these steps before?"

- "What did you learn from this description of physical progression?"

- "How will this knowledge help you establish good physical boundaries?"

Remind the group about the story of Joseph and Potiphar's wife.

- "What insights did you pick up regarding physical boundaries from Joseph's character and actions?"

- "What can you do when your physical boundaries are questioned or threatened?"

Discuss the statement, "You should only go as far physically with a boy as you would if your father were present."

- "What do you think about this idea?"

- "How does your dad watch over your virtue? How can you discuss the area of setting boundaries with him?"

Whether or not their dads help them guard their virtue, every girl has a heavenly Father who watches over them. Nothing is hidden from Him.

- "How does remembering this affect your physical boundaries with a guy?"

Discuss the definition of lust and how everyone struggles with it. Discuss how acting and dressing modestly are practical ways girls can help guys resist lust and sexual temptation.

End the session by praying that the girls will set good boundaries for their girl/guy relationships. Pray for anyone who has struggled with this area.

Encourage them to read the next chapter so they'll be prepared for the next session.

Chapter 8: I've Messed Up, Now What?

Materials

- blank paper

- writing utensils

- garbage container for paper

At the beginning of the session, distribute a blank piece of paper and pen to each girl. Ask them to think of something in their past they are ashamed of and write it on the paper. Assure them that what they write will not be seen by anyone else. Now have them fold the paper in quarters and hold it during the rest of the group time.

Have the girls open their Bibles to Joshua 2. Read the story of Rahab aloud, going around the group or having one person do it.

Ask the girls to read the chapter again silently, underlining the verses that speak to them. Then have each student share thoughts from Rahab's story that were either new to them or spoke to their hearts.

- "If God forgets our sin when we ask Him for forgiveness, why is it so hard for us to forget it when someone hurts us?"

- "What is the difference between forgetting and forgiving?"

Encourage the girls to discuss Ann's story about getting pregnant in high school and what they learned from her experience. Include how they would treat someone in their group if they learned she was pregnant.

Spend a few moments discussing repentance, including the definition and why it's the key to forgiveness.

Place a trash can in the middle of the group. Ask each student to take a moment to think about what they wrote on their papers. Talk about holding on to the sin or releasing it. Ask the girls to bow their heads and silently spend time asking the Lord to forgive them of the sin and to thank Him for forgetting the sin. While their heads are bowed, read 1 John 1:9: "If we confess our sins, [God] is faithful and just and will forgive us our sins and purify us from all unrighteousness."

Finish the session by instructing the girls to toss their papers in the trash as a symbol that God has forgiven them so the sin is no longer in their lives.

Chapter 9: The Label to Avoid

Materials: If possible, have women come to teach about using makeup and finding clothing that is modest and stylish. Do makeup makeovers after the meeting.

Discuss how perception isn't always true even though it looks real.

- "What do people assume about other people because of the way they are dressed?"

- "If someone sees you for the first time, what impression will she get?"

- "What do you think about modesty? What is the purpose of modesty?"

- "Is modesty an issue at school? At church? Anywhere else?"

- "How can you tell if you're dressed modestly or not?"

- "How can you encourage each other in this area and hold each other accountable?"

Read Colossians 3:5-17 aloud. Ask the girls to identify areas in their lives that need to go into the trash. Then have them identify behaviors they want to "put on."

- "What actions will you take this week to put on those traits?"

Talk about girls calling guys for dates.

- "Would you call a guy to ask him out on a date? Why or why not?"

Discuss whether guys should take the lead by asking the girl out.

Being careful to avoid mentioning specific girls or situations and keeping the discussion on track, discuss healthy boundaries for how girls interact with boys. Talk about pursuit, appropriate physical contact, and public displays of affection.

Talk about what the girls learned from reading about Samson and Delilah. Include how what they read can apply to their own relationships.

Have the girls turn to the media chart at the end of chapter 10. Ask them to fill it out during the next week so you can discuss the results at the next session.

Close the session in prayer.

Have fun doing makeup makeovers and discussing clothes.

Chapter 10: Reality TV Dating v. Real-Life Dating

Spend time evaluating the media charts the girls filled out during the previous week.

- "Were you surprised at how much time you spent in any one area?"

- "Are there some changes you want or need to make?"

- "Have you considered replacing some of your social media time with more profitable pursuits? What would you do instead?"

- "Do you need to spend more face-to-face time with people? If so, what will you do this week to do that?"

Compare Robin and Lauren's stories about their media experiences. How can media be used to promote the gospel and God's values?

Read the first chapter of the book of Daniel together.

- "What happened to Daniel and his friends? What things changed?"

- "What was different about Babylon?"

- "How would you feel if you were in Daniel's situation?"

Read Daniel 1:8.

- "What did Daniel and his friends resolve not to do? Why was this important to them?"

- "What were the results of their taking a stand?" (See Daniel 1:15-17.)

- "How does this taking a stand relate to your situation today?"

- "How can you avoid doing the things in today's culture that go against God's way?"

Define "apologetics." After discussion, tell them apologetics simply means "defending your faith."

- "How can you defend your faith against the standards of today's culture?"

- "What can you do to be able to give a good defense for the gospel of Jesus Christ?"

Have the girls review the verses cited in the chapter and pick one out to read aloud.

End the session praying for God's wisdom to be made clear to everyone.

Chapter 11: The One Man Who Will Never Let You Down

Have the girls toss out names of romantic movies. Discuss the common themes, such as guy meets girl, some kind of conflict, conflict resolution, and a happy ending.

- "How important is it to have a happy ending?"

- "Does the guy in the movie pursue the girl? Is that attractive to you? Why or why not?"

Have the girls look up the following passages about Jesus' interacting with women.

Matthew 9:20-22 and *Mark 5:24-34*. Describe this woman's situation.

- "Why was it important for her to touch Jesus?"

- "How did she respond when Jesus asked who touched Him?"

- "What did Jesus say when He healed her?"

- "Do you need Jesus to heal you today?"

Matthew 15:21-28 and *Mark 7:24-30*. Describe this woman's situation.

- "How did Jesus respond at first to her requests?"

- "Does this seem harsh to you?"

- "What do these verses say about the place of women in that day?"

- "What was Jesus' response to the woman's reply to His comment?"

- "Do you easily give up when you bring your requests to God and don't seem to get an answer right away? What can you do or say to be more persistent in your requests?"

Luke 7:36-50. Describe this woman's situation.

- "What act of service did she do for Jesus?"

- "Why do you think she wept?"

- "How did Jesus treat this woman compared to the way others treated her?"

- "What does this say about Jesus' care for women?"

- "Why were her sins forgiven?"

Luke 10:38-42. Describe these two women.

- "In what ways are these two women different?"

- "Why did Jesus praise Mary's actions?"

- "How will you sit at Jesus' feet this week?"

John 4:5-42. Describe this woman's situation.

- "Why was it unusual for Jesus to speak to this woman?"

- "What did Jesus mean when He offered the woman 'living water'?"

- "What happened in her community when she shared about Jesus?"

- "How are you sharing Christ with others?"

Matthew 28:1-8, Mark 16:1-8, and *Luke 24:1-10.* Describe the situation.

- "Why do you think Jesus appeared to women first after His resurrection?"

- "What was their response?"

- "How did their testimony influence history?"

• "How has Jesus revealed His resurrection power in your life?"

John 8:1-11. Describe this woman's situation.

- "What were the Pharisees about to do to her?"

- "What was Jesus' reaction?"

- "What instructions did Jesus give the woman?"

Now discuss all the passages.

- "Were any of these women married?"

- "Did Jesus pursue them? If yes, was it romantically or spiritually?"

- "How was Jesus the perfect man for each of them?"

- "In what ways did each of them suffer?"

- "How did Jesus meet their needs?"

- "How can you help people who are suffering?"

Ask for volunteers to share their testimonies with the group.

Ask the girls to bow their heads to pray silently. Then, while their heads are bowed, invite anyone who wants to pray to accept Jesus to look at you. Nod at each one and acknowledge them by saying "good." Lead everyone in a prayer of repentance. After the group dismisses, reach out to the girls who indicated they wanted to accept Jesus. Follow up with them later in the week to encourage them to make their decision public and learn more about Jesus.

If all the students in your group are Christians, ask them to pray silently for someone they know who needs to know Christ. Encourage students to boldly continue praying for their lost friends and to look for opportunities to share the gospel.

NOTES

Chapter 2: Mirror, Mirror of My Heart

1. http://www.education.com/reference/article/how-magazines-affect-body-image/ with research from http://cmch.tv/mentors/fullRecord.asp?id=2055, accessed 11/17/2011.

2. http://www.dailymail.co.uk/news/article-491741/British-women-look-mirror-71-times-day-survey-reveals.html, accessed 11/22/2011.

Chapter 3: Evolution of Dating

1. http://mashable.com/2010/10/14/nielsen-texting-stats/, accessed 11/22/2011.

Chapter 4: Boy Friends and Boyfriends

1. Read more at http://www.bibletools.org/index.cfm/fuseaction/Topical.show/RTD/cgg/ID/2779/Defraud.htm#ixzz1ePfOnYnw, accessed 11/22/2011.

2. Chad Eastham, *The Truth About Dating, Love and Just Being Friends* (Nashville: Thomas Nelson, 2011), 108.

Chapter 7: How Far Is Too Far?

1. James Dobson, *Love for a Lifetime* (Portland, OR: Multnomah Press, 1987), 32-34.

2. http://thechart.blogs.cnn.com/2011/04/05/teen-pregnancy-rate-lowest-in-two-decades/, accessed 12/9/2011.

3. http://www.bhg.com/health-family/parenting-skills/teen-challenges/stds-teens-a-reality-check/, accessed 12/9/2011.

4. http://www.heritage.org/research/reports/2003/06/sexually-active-teenag-ers-are-more-likely-to-be-depressed, accessed 12/9/2011.

Chapter 8: I've Messed Up, Now What?

1. Liz Curtis Higgs, *Bad Girls of the Bible* (Colorado Springs: Waterbrook Press, 1999), 159.

2. Ibid., 165.

3. Created by LifeWay Christian Resources of the Southern Baptist Conven-tion, "True Love Waits" is designed to encourage moral purity by adhering to biblical principles. This youth-based international campaign established in 1993 utilizes positive peer pressure by encouraging those who make a commitment to refrain from premarital sex to challenge their peers to do the same.

Chapter 10: Reality TV Dating v. Real-Life Dating

1. http://depts.washington.edu/thmedia/view.cgi?section=medialiteracy&page=fastfacts, accessed 12/18/2011.

About Robin

Robin Marsh is an Emmy-nominated, national award-winning journalist. She's received many accolades, including excellence in feature reporting from the National Academy of Television Journalists, honors from the Society of Professional Journalists, and "Oklahoma's Journalist of the Year." The Girl Scouts honored Robin as a "Woman of Distinction." Her series on breast cancer is on display at the Museum of Broadcast Communications (Chicago).

A veteran journalist on television news for almost 30 years, Robin currently anchors the morning news on KWTV-News 9, the CBS affiliate in Oklahoma City. She served on the board of directors for the Baptist Foundation of Oklahoma and supports numerous charities.

Using her influence in broadcasting to open doors to share Jesus, Robin enjoys being a motivational speaker and sharing about Jesus Christ. She leads retreats for girls and women, and a personal highlight was sharing her testimony with 7000 students at Falls Creek Church Camp in Oklahoma.

Robin is an accomplished horsewoman who competed in rodeos and Oklahoma "play days." She and her husband, Keith, have an 11-year-old son.

About Lauren

Lauren Nelson was crowned Miss America in 2007. She received the prestigious TOYA Award, being honored as one of the "Ten Outstanding Young Americans" by the United States Junior Chamber Organization in 2008. During her tenure as Miss America, Lauren traveled the United States to promote Internet safety for children. She lends her name to numerous organizations but has a special place in her heart for the Children's Miracle Network.

A graduate of the University of Central Oklahoma, Lauren holds a degree in public relations. She currently is a news anchor for KWTV-News 9, the CBS affiliate in Oklahoma City. She also speaks at numerous women's events, youth retreats, and charity functions.

An accomplished singer and performer, Lauren costarred with Shirley Jones and Patrick Cassidy in "Carousel" and sang the national anthem and other songs for several professional sporting events.

Lauren and her husband, Randy, lead worship Sunday mornings (contemporary service) and Wednesday nights for the youth at their church.

God, Girls, and Getting Connected
Robin Marsh and
Lauren Nelson

*Wish your questions about life, faith,
and relationships could be answered
as fast as a text message to your best friend?*

Here's the great news: God's text message—the Bible—is full of immediate personal messages and answers for you. And these straight-talk
devotions highlight what matters most to you with spiritual apps to help
you connect with and embrace your...

> **G**od. Who knows and cares about your every
> need and dream.
>
> **I**dentity. What makes you unique and
> wonderful.
>
> **R**elationships. How to deal with family, boys,
> and even girlfriend drama.
>
> **L**ife. Why living out a bold faith leads to joy
> and purpose.

Each quick and meaningful devotion is in tune with what your heart
longs to hear. In an instant, you'll discover why accepting God's call is
the best and most exciting decision you'll *ever* make.

• • • • •

**Discover more at
www.withunveiledfaces.com**

● ● ● ● ●

Authentic. **Real.** *Transparent.*

Unveiled is the ministry of two passionate women.
Miss America 2007 Lauren Nelson and award-winning
television news anchor Robin Marsh team up to
reach teen girls with the good news of Jesus Christ.

The mission of Unveiled Ministries is to connect
young women spiritually and socially so they can
become confident women of God.

MINISTRIES

*And we all, who with unveiled faces reflect the Lord's glory,
are being transformed into his image with ever-increasing
glory, which comes from the Lord, who is the Spirit.*

2 CORINTHIANS 3:18

● ● ● ● ●

Connect with Robin & Lauren

www.withunveiledfaces.com
Twitter: *@withunveiled*

info@withunveiledfaces.com
Facebook: *withunveiledfaces*